The Rain Falls On The Just And The Unjust

Donna Louis

Dedication

To my soul mate Patrick who is my rock and always there for me. I am so grateful that God blessed me to share my life with you. I'll love you always.

Acknowledgments

To God, my heavenly father, who constantly blesses me with the anointing to write and remind his children that he loves them all dearly and is with them every step of their lives. God, thank you for ordering and directing our steps daily and always blessing us.

To Don, you are truly the master blaster. Thank you for encouraging me to write this book. It was a pleasure to write. I will ever be grateful to you for all you have done and continue to do for me.

To all the modern-day people who have been mentioned in this book for being tremendous examples for the rest of us to see how you continued to forge through and stay in the game even when the rain fell on your lives.

Introduction

When the rain falls, it doesn't just pick, choose, and refuse who it wants to dump on. In Florida where I live it is very common to have huge downpours for about 10-15 minutes and then the sun starts to shine again. It is also very prevalent where you can be driving in one area and as soon as you go several blocks there is no rain. I have also seen it where you are out walking, and it is raining on one side of the street and the other side is completely dry. WOW! The wonders of God. However, I have never seen it where it rains on the first house on the block skips the next one and then it is raining on the third house.

We just encountered this with Hurricane Ian. It hit our state as a Category 4 and has caused quite a lot of devastation. I can guarantee you that the rains fell on believers of God as well as non-believers. The Bible says that "For there is no respect of persons with God." –Romans 2:11. Therefore we as believers of God must realize that just because we do what is godly that does not mean we are exempt from trials.

I read this the other day "Never complain about the difficulties in life; because a Director (God) always gives the hardest roles to his best actors!" Now I realize that this may not put a smile on a believer's face, but the same message is in the Bible in the book of James. "My brethren, count it all joy when you fall into divers temptations, knowing this, that the trying of your faith worketh patience. But let patience have her perfect work, that ye may be perfect and entire, wanting nothing." -James 1:2-4. Now for those of you like me where patience is not one of your greatest assets you don't like hearing this. I remember when I first encountered these verses in the Bible, I was not happy. I clearly remember telling God you said you knew me before you formed me so that means you were good with who I was. For those of you who do not have a strong gift of being an exhorter you may be saying, how can she be talking to God like that? Don't worry God understands me. For those of you who have this gift you know where I'm coming from! However, God is always expecting us to improve daily. When you are a new believer, you can only take the word in small doses just like a newborn baby drinks milk. However, after you have had some experiences in life with God and he has shown his goodness to you then the stakes get raised and he expects you to trust him more when you encounter fiery trials. This journey of life is a series of test and as we grow in God, he expects us to pass these tests. Later in the book you will read all about these tests. However, let me give you an FYI now: if you don't pass the test God has a real sense of humor and will continue to repeat the same test repeatedly until you pass them.

"Being confident of this, that he who began a good work in you will carry it on till completion until the day of Christ Jesus." – Philippians 1:6. The Apostle Paul when he was nearing the end of his life he wrote to the church in Philippi and tried to encourage them to stay strong even though the work God was doing in their lives was not pleasant. The tests and trials that God was putting the people through was meant to strengthen them and for them to become more dependent on God. As believers God created us to bring unbelievers to Christ and to have daily fellowship with him. When God feels you drifting away, he will mobilize all his angels and start to tow you back to him.

"That ye may be the children of your Father which is in heaven: for he maketh his sun to rise on the evil and on the good, and sendeth rain on the just and the unjust." –Matthew 5:45. When you are going through season after season of rain just remember God built you and you are stronger than you think. Also remember the things that you are praying for that you still don't see being manifested if it's taking a long time that is because God has something bigger and better for you than what you were praying for.

Contents

Chapter 1

What Does The Bible Say About Rain?

They reference rain as a blessing given to you after a drought. The Bible has quite a lot to say about rain and not just regarding harvesting crops.

Sow to yourselves in righteousness, reap in mercy; break up your fallow ground: for it is time to seek the Lord, till he come and rain righteousness upon you. –Hosea 10:12

"You heavens above, rain down my righteousness; let the clouds shower it down. Let the earth open wide, let salvation spring up, let righteousness flourish with it; I, the LORD, have created it."–Isaiah 45:8

Do any of the worthless idols of the nation bring rain? Do the skies themselves send down showers? No, it is you, LORD our God. Therefore, our hope is in you, for you are the one who does all this. –Jeremiah 14:22.

As the rain and the snow come down from heaven, and do not return to it without watering the earth and making it bud and flourish, so that it yields seed for the sower and bread for the eater, -Isaiah 55:10

I will send you rain in its season, and the ground will yield its crops and the trees their fruit. –Leviticus 26:4

We Are All Created Equal

It is very important that we all remember that we are all created equal. One of our greatest leaders Dr. Martin Luther King Jr. referenced this when he spoke at Ebenezer Baptist Church in Atlanta GA back in 1965 and reminded us of The Declaration of Independence when he recited these words, "We hold these truths to be self-evident, that all men are created equal, that they are endowed by God, Creator, with certain inalienable rights, that among these are life, liberty and the pursuit of happiness."

Yes, we may all look different regarding color, shape, sizes etc. but when God created us, he made all of us the same. This is clearly enunciated in the Bible when Peter says, "Then Peter opened his mouth, and said, "Of a truth I perceive God is no respecter of persons."–Acts 10:34

Therefore, this Bible verse should not throw Christians and believers in God, Jesus, & The Holy Spirit off when it says, "That ye may be the children of your Father which is in heaven: for he maketh his sun to rise on the evil and on the good, and sendeth rain on the just and on the unjust." -Matthew 5:45. God loves all his creations the same. That is why we should not become indignant because we encounter challengers, trials, and testing periods. We should not become haughty and believe that because we go to church, read our Bible, sing in the choir, volunteer to serve at church functions, visit the sick and shut in at the hospitals, give of our tithes and offerings, etc. that no bad things should befall us. I just read the other day "Never complain about the difficulties in life; because the Director (GOD) always gives the hardest roles to his best actors!"

Don't Panic Instead Pray

Panicking just brings a flood of negative emotions, and that will block your blessings from God. Your prayer life needs to be simple and not a spectacle for the world to see. Why do I say this? That is what the Bible says, "But thou, when thou prayest, enter into thy closet, and when thou hast shut thy door, pray to thy

Father which is in secret; and thy Father which seeth in secret shall reward thee openly."–Matthew 6:6.

If you feel you are panicking or becoming fearful, refer to the following Bible verses:

"So that we may boldly say, The Lord is my helper, and I will not fear what man shall do unto me." –Hebrews 13:6

"Be careful for nothing, but in everything by prayer and supplication with thanksgiving let your requests be made known unto God." –Philippians 4:6

"For God hath not given us the spirit of fear, but of power, and of love, and of a sound mind." –2 Timothy 1:7.

"Ye are of God, little children, and have overcome them: because greater is he that is in you, than he that is in the world." -1 John 4:4

"For I the LORD thy God will hold thy right hand, saying unto thee, Fear not; I will help thee." –Isaiah 41:13

"And fear not them which kill the body but are not able to kill the soul: but rather fear him which is able to destroy both soul and body in hell." –Matthew 10:28

Many people complicate their prayer life unnecessarily, and this is not what God wants. Keep it simple. "He gave us all a great example of this, after this manner, therefore, pray ye: Our Father which art in heaven, Hallowed be thy name. Thy kingdom come, thy will be done in earth, as it is in heaven. Give us this day our daily bread. And forgive us our debts, as we forgive our debtors. And lead us not into temptation but deliver us from evil: For thine is the kingdom, and the power, and the glory, forever. Amen."–Matthew 6:6-13.

Your prayer life should include:

Devotion–We need to let God know that we are dedicated and loyal to him.

He did that for us when he sent Jesus to the cross for all of us. "And whatsoever ye do in word or deed, do all in the name of the Lord Jesus, giving thanks to God and the Father by him." –Colossians 3:17.

Confession–We need to confess our sins to God and ask for forgiveness. "As it is written, there is none righteous, no, not one: There is none that understandeth, there is none that seeketh after God. They are all gone out of the way, they are together become unprofitable; there is none that doeth good, no, not one." -Romans 3:10-12.

Gratitude–We all need to give thanks to God daily for every gift we receive. Water to drink, food to eat, use of our senses, sunshine, etc. "In everything give thanks: for this is the will of God in Christ Jesus concerning you." -1 Thessalonians 5:18. "O give thanks unto the Lord; for he is good: for his mercy endureth forever." –Psalms 136:1. "Praise ye the Lord. O give thanks unto the Lord; for he is good: for his mercy endureth forever." –Psalms 106:1. "But thanks be to God, which giveth us the victory through our Lord Jesus Christ." -1 Corinthians 15:57.

Praise-When we praise God, the heavens are happy. Praise is a vital part of a life surrendered to God, and it gives credit where credit is due. "Praise ye the Lord. Praise God in his sanctuary: praise him in the firmament of his power. Praise him for his mighty acts: praise him according to his excellent greatness. Praise him with the sound of the trumpet: praise him with the psaltery and harp. Praise him with the timbrel and dance: praise him with stringed instruments and organs. Praise him upon the loud cymbals: praise him upon the high-sounding cymbals. Let everything that hath breath praise the Lord. Praise ye the Lord." –Psalm 150:1-6. "By him, therefore, let us offer the sacrifice of praise to God continually, the fruit of our lips giving thanks to his name." –Hebrews 13:15.

Rollercoaster Of Life

It doesn't matter how much reverence you show to God, there will be times in your life when you encounter rainy seasons. However, when you continue to show esteem to God, once the winds and storms have passed, you will still stand tall. "Wherefore take unto you the whole armour of God, that ye may be able to withstand in the evil day, and having done all, to stand."–Ephesians 6:13.

Rollercoaster rides in amusement parks differ from the rollercoaster storms of life, but there is a valuable lesson to learn from the rollercoasters in the amusement parks. Roller Coasters have become one of the mandatory rides for the thrill-seekers whenever they visit amusement parks. They have become an engineering marvel, and have been constructed to be taller, faster, and wilder than ever. They say that the language of love is French, so for thrill-seekers it is called "amateurs de sensations fortes".

Why is it, though we climb into the roller coaster giddy, sweaty, pumped with adrenaline and faith that the ride will be exceptional? We never have wavering faith that our feet will never land safely on solid ground within 3 1/2 to 4 minutes after the inception of the ride. So, if we are so confident and stable and grounded in our faith in a man-made steel object, why is our faith so flimsy in our creator?

In Genesis 1:1 it says, "In the beginning, God created the heaven and the earth". In Genesis 1:26 it states, "And GOD said, let us make man in our image, after our likeness." So, I have a question for you to ponder if GOD created man and endowed him with powerful knowledge to create roller coasters shouldn't we have the strongest unfailing faith in GOD.

A Blissful Life Is Not Guaranteed

When we were born as babies, we were pampered, comforted, loved, cradled, fed, changed, and as we grew, we were given every creature comfort possible. No wonder we thought that life would be a constant cycle of bliss.

Reality set in as we grew older. Going to school was a perfect example. Sometimes it was difficult to make friends. We didn't always get the best grades on our tests and homework assignments. Then there were those of us that were unfortunately bullied.

As we grew into adults, then the veritable maze began. We thought once we graduated, we would find the perfect job or open our dream business and work there until retirement. We would find the perfect spouse, have a couple of kids if we chose, purchase a home, a couple of cars, and possibly have a pet or two and life would be great.

Surprise! A Blissful Life Is Not Guaranteed. As adults, we all have, at one point or another, faced some of these issues:

Being laid off or fired from a job

Lost a loved one to death

Struggled or still struggling with health issues

Divorce

Lost a business that you owned

Been involved in an accident of some type

Had to file Bankruptcy

I know there are many things that I have left off this list. We need to remember that Jesus did not have a blissful life when he was here on earth, either. Jesus endured physical torment, emotional trauma, and spiritual agony, but he never wavered. Gods got this, he's got you just lean in and trust him when the storms of life come. Remember, if he saved Peter from drowning, he will save you as well.

Chapter 2

What Is A Core Foundation For God To Show Out In Your Life?

A core is a central or foundational part, usually distinct from the enveloping part by a difference in nature. A foundation is an underlying base or support; a body or ground upon which something is built up or overlaid. - https://www.merriam-webster.com/dictionary.

When Jesus was here on earth, what was he constantly in the habit of doing always? Praying. So, this is your core foundation. Prayer is the direct communication line to God. He is ordering and directing all our steps. Therefore, he is Alpha & Omega. God created us to be in fellowship with him. "God is faithful, by whom ye were called unto the fellowship of his Son Jesus Christ our Lord."–1 Corinthians 1:9.

Along with God being Alpha & Omega, he is also the greatest maestro/conductor of all time. Maestro - a master usually in an art; especially an eminent composer, conductor, or teacher of music. - https://www.merriam-webster.com/dictionary/maestro

Conductor - the leader of a musical ensemble, an orchestra conductor - https://www.merriam-webster.com/dictionary/conductor

An article titled "Top 10 Qualities of an Effective Band or Orchestra Conductor" Curated from SBO Magazine–by Harvey Rachlin states that these are the qualities of a good orchestra leader is they should have integrity, competence and passion, be committed to the job, be a good communicator, be respectful, be able to make good decisions, and be knowledgeable and confident. One of the greatest conductors–maestro's ever was Leonard Bernstein. He was an American conductor, composer, pianist, music educator, author, and humanitarian. Among the most important conductors of his time, he was also the first American conductor to receive international acclaim. As a composer, he wrote in many styles, including symphonic and orchestral music, ballet, film and theatre music, choral works, opera, chamber music and works for the piano. His best-known work is the Broadway musical West Side Story, which continues to be regularly performed worldwide. - https://en.wikipedia.org/wiki/Leonard_Bernstein.

Looking at the above qualities of an excellent conductor, maestro, we see the similarities to God. The essence of integrity is him. He is Alpha & Omega and created and completed this world in six days, so he is very competent and above all, his passion for all of us and sending Jesus to the cross to die for our sins because he loves us so much. He is so committed to his work with this world that even though he destroyed it with flood waters, he still asked Noah to put two of every animal in the ark along with Noah's entire family to repopulate the world after the flood waters dried up off the earth. God is extremely committed to his job and is an excellent communicator since the beginning, down to Moses, Abraham, Joseph, Jacob, and all the other giants in the Bible. God gave us all free will and allowed us the opportunity to make our own choices, even though most were wrong. He respected what we chose. God never makes mistakes and makes excellent decisions and is extremely knowledgeable and confident in what he has planned and executed. With all of this, why do we find it so hard to trust and believe in him?

The same way in which a conductor–maestro directs an orchestra, that is the way God directs our steps. He knows the plans that he has for us and the glorious future he wants to give us. If we would just communicate with God via prayer and spend time in his presence, since his greatest desire is to have fellowship with us, we would enjoy the greatest lives even in the challenging times when the rain falls on the just and the unjust. What we need to do is just like the patrons of the arts and music do when they attend a concert. We just need to settle into our seats, get comfortable, and enjoy the presentation. If we would just allow God to keep control of the baton, the same way the conductor of an orchestra does, we would have a wonderful life.

The Eagle

"Bless the Lord, O my soul: and all that is within me, bless his holy name. Bless the Lord, O my soul, and forget not all his benefits: Who forgiveth all thine iniquities; who healeth all thy diseases; Who redeemeth thy life from destruction; who crowneth thee with lovingkindness and tender mercies; Who satisfieth thy mouth with good things; so that thy youth is renewed like the eagle's." -Psalm 103:1-5.

When eagles come to mind, people commonly imagine some enormous hunter soaring above wide-open spaces on outsized wings. What makes this bird so important and symbolic to humanity is its characteristics.

Eagles have tremendous vision. God designed their eyes to scan and cover long-distance and to concentrate and have lucidity. They are able to see other eagles flying from 50 miles away. Successful people have a vision. "If art is to nourish the roots of our culture, society must set the artist free to follow his vision wherever it takes him" - John F. Kennedy. Where there is no vision, the people perish: but he that keepeth the law, happy is he. -Proverbs 29:18.

Eagles are fearless - Eagle never yield their power to the physical magnitude or toughness of its prey. Eagles always stand strong and fight to conquer their prey or keep their area. Successful people are fearless. "I learned that courage was not the absence of fear, but the triumph over it. The brave man is not he who does not feel afraid, but he who conquers that fear." - Nelson Mandela. If thou faint in the day of adversity, thy strength is small. -Proverbs 24:10.

Eagles are aggressive. Eagles are known for their aggression. The only birds that like flying in the storm are eagles. When all other birds try to flee from the storm and hide, eagles fly into it and will use the wind of the storm to rise higher in a matter of seconds. People rise to greater heights when they take up challenges head-on without running away from them. "Love not sleep, lest thou come to poverty; open thine eyes, and thou shalt be satisfied with bread." - Proverbs 20:13. "Put on the whole armour of God, that ye may be able to stand against the wiles of the devil." -Ephesians 6:11.

Eagles know patience and when to get silent - Eagle have the longest lifespan out of its species. They are able to live up to 70 years. However, for them to reach this age, eagles must make a tough decision. When they reach their 40', their extended and pliant talons are incapable of seizing prey, which is considered their food. Their extended and piercing beak is no longer in its original state of being straight. Because of its advanced years, it has become decrepit and because of the substantial weight of its wings, mostly in part of their bulky feathers, sticks to the eagle's chest and make it arduous to fly. At this point, the eagles must choose to prepare to pass away or to endure affliction which has a duration which lasts 150 days. The procedure demands the eagle fly to a very high mountaintop and rest on a nest. Upon arrival, the eagle must strike its beak continually against a rock until it is removed. Once that is completed, the eagle must wait for a new beak to manifest, and then the eagle will pluck out the talons. When the manifested talons mature, the eagle then removes its decrepit feathers. Eventually, once five months have passed, the powerful eagle soars into flight and has added another 30 years to its life. "You can learn more from silence than all the voices in the world." - Madame Guyon. "For ye have need of patience, that, after ye have done the will of God, ye might receive the promise." - Hebrews 10:36.

These are just some characteristics of an eagle. So, should we pattern the characteristics of an eagle? "But they that wait upon the Lord shall renew their strength; they shall mount up with wings as eagles; they shall run, and not be weary, and they shall walk, and not faint." -Isaiah 40:31

Take Your Eyes Off Yourself–Be Someone's Miracle

"I have shewed you all things, how that so labouring ye ought to support the weak, and to remember the words of the Lord Jesus, how he said, it is more blessed to give than to receive." –Acts 20:35.

The quickest way to bring about your own miracle is to become a miracle in someone else's life. Now, because we are human, and we have a selfish nature, we want our own needs to be met and satisfied before we attempt to help anyone else. However, this is not the way our heavenly father wants us to be. The same way that God created us to be in fellowship with him constantly, he also wants us to be in fellowship with others. Our miracle is tied into providing someone else with their miracle. "Bear ye one another's burdens, and so fulfil the law of Christ." -Galatians 6:2

When we have our challenges and struggles, the last thing we want to do is help someone else. We believe that as soon as all is well with us, then we might assist others. This is wrong, selfish thinking. My husband and I attended a "Night of Hope" event with Joel Osteen six years ago and were so moved by the number of people that became a part of an organization named World Vision where you can sponsor a child. There were hundreds of people in line holding their card with the picture of the child they were given to sponsor including my husband and me. My husband jokingly said to me, "it's taken you 31 years of marriage to finally give me a son." I can tell you it is a rewarding experience to help someone else. If you don't believe me, here are quotes from other people:

"Those who are happiest are those who do the most for others." - Booker T. Washington

"I prefer death to tiredness. I am never tired of serving others." - Leonardo da Vinci

"We rise by lifting others." - Robert Ingersall

"It is literally true that you can succeed best and quicker by helping others to succeed." - Napolean Hill

"We make a living by what we get, but we make a life by what we give." - Winston Churchill

"You have not lived today until you have done something for someone who can never repay you." - John Bunyan

There was a story on the internet about a woman named Caroline Boudreaux, who had all the material things she wanted living in Austin TX but was dissatisfied with her life. She took a year off from work to travel the world and came across an orphanage in rural India. There was not enough food for the children there to eat and poor living conditions. She was so moved by what she saw she created an organization called The Miracle Foundation. They have now existed over 22 years and have helped children. Caroline is now satisfied with her life.

Let's look at what God's word says about helping others:

Hebrews 13:16 – "But to do good and to communicate forget not: for with such sacrifices, God is well pleased".

Philippians 2:4 – "Look not every man on his own things, but every man also on the things of others."

Luke 6:38 – "Give, and it shall be given unto you; good measure, pressed down, and shaken together, and running over, shall men give into your bosom. For with the same measure that ye mete withal it shall be measured to you again."

1 John 3:17 – "But whoso hath this world's good, and seeth his brother have need, and shutteth up his bowels [of compassion] from him, how dwelleth the love of God in him?"

Matthew 25:35-40 – "For I was an hungred, and ye gave me meat: I was thirsty, and ye gave me drink: I was a stranger, and ye took me in."

James 2:14-17 – "What [doth it] profit, my brethren, though a man say he hath faith, and have not works? Can faith save him?"

Galatians 6:2 – "Bear ye one another's burdens, and so fulfil the law of Christ."

John 15:12 – "This is my commandment, that ye love one another, as I have loved you."

Matthew 5:16 – "Let your light so shine before men, that they may see your good works, and glorify your Father which is in heaven."

Proverbs 19:17 – "He that hath pity upon the poor lendeth unto the LORD; and that which he hath given will he pay him again."

Proverbs 22:9 – "He that hath a bountiful eye shall be blessed; for he giveth of his bread to the poor."

Matthew 5:42 – "Give to him that asketh thee, and from him that would borrow of thee turn not thou away."

Romans 15:1 – "We then that are strong ought to bear the infirmities of the weak, and not to please ourselves."

YOU WANT TO ACCELERATE YOUR MIRACLE-----BE SOMEONE'S ELSE'S MIRACLE!

Back To God

That time of year has come upon us once again, "Back to School." The clothes shopping, books and backpacks, pencils pens, computers, iPad, index cards, laptops, etc. What would happen if adults, young people, parents would decide to go Back to God?

So many of us have turned away from God because our lives are not all wine and roses like we assumed it should be. Be careful when you assume because of what it means. Break down the word and you can figure out what it says!

However, it is very sad when Christians and believers turn their back on God. If Jesus went through trials and challenges and was tempted what makes you think you are EXEMPT? There are many Christians who have wandered away from the Lord. We have so much to gain by being faithful to the Lord. Rest assured that God wants you back and is keen to see it happen. Being a Christian is all about having a relationship with God. Like any relationship, that means listening and talking to God. So as for what you should do first, I think listening to God is a great place to start. And as for who to talk to first, I think talking to God is a great place to start. What a magnificent picture of God's love for us! You want to come back to God - and it fills God with compassion for you - He wants to welcome you home. And he wants to celebrate. Listen to God - and God says, 'Welcome home.'

When we go away from God, the thing God desires most is that we return. In Luke 15:1-7, Jesus spoke a parable. He says that a man had 100 sheep and one was lost who then is found; there is more rejoicing in heaven over the one than over the 99 who never became lost. If we apply the parable as Jesus intended it to be applied, we are His sheep. If one of us goes astray and becomes lost, there is great rejoicing when that one returns to Christ. Jesus is the key to any of us coming back to God. Jesus is God's way of making us worthy to be called God's sons - God's children. By trusting in Jesus, we can be God's children again - we can have a relationship with God as our Heavenly Father. Satan wants us to believe that once we have fallen away, there is no way back. But this is not true. In Luke 15:7, Jesus says, "I say to you that likewise there will be more joy in heaven over one sinner that repents than over ninety-nine just persons who need no repentance." Then Jesus continues in verse 10, saying, "Likewise, I say to you, there is joy in the presence of the angels of God over one sinner who repents." When we repent and come back, all of heaven rejoices.

Don't allow your trials and hardships, and disappointments to take you away from God. Don't think that just because you are living a holier life than others that you are exempt from struggles and test. They come to all of us. We all have one time, or another strayed from GOD. Let's look at Bible history: Abraham went away from God and journeyed to Egypt. But God did not abandon him, and God sought him in Egypt and brought him back to the Promised Land. Jacob went away from God and told lies, cheated, and treated his father and brother badly. But God did not abandon him. When Jacob returned, God was there for him. The ten sons of Jacob went away from God and treated Joseph badly. But when they were old, they returned to God and were blessed by Him and became the patriarchs of Israel. Aaron went away from God and made a golden calf for an idol. But when he returned, God accepted him and speaks highly of him in Scripture. David abandoned God, committed adultery with Bathsheba, killed Bathsheba's husband, and stayed away from God for about nine months. But when confronted by Nathan the prophet, David returned to God and God restored David to a proper standing with Him. Perhaps the greatest example is Manasseh. Manasseh had a godly father in King Hezekiah. But Manasseh turned against God and did great atrocities. He was very evil (2 Chronicles 33:1-9). But when Manasseh turned back to God, God restored him (2 Chronicles 33:10-20).

So do not think that your actions have made you a lost cause in God's eyes or that the Lord is threw with you because you are just "too evil." The Bible says that wherever sin exists, God's grace meaning His free forgiveness is greater. No one has sinned so much that they are no longer eligible for Heaven. Yes, the rain falls on the just and the unjust, but you are God's masterpiece, and he loves you and is ordering your steps and will make you triumph!

Psalm 34

The Bible is the most read book of all books that have ever been created. It is stockpiled with so much wisdom, love, examples of how we should live our lives and show reverence to God. The Book of Psalms is one of the most read books in the Bible, especially from the Old Testament.

The Hebrew word for Psalms in Tehilim means "Praise". Psalm 34 is called "A Psalm of David". It references when David changed his behavior before Abimelech, who drove him away, and he departed.

Psalm 34 is a Psalm that can be very encouraging to you when you feel like the walls of life are closing in on you and you have no way out. The times when if anything that can go wrong, it does. The times when you are so overwhelmed when the tears just flow and laughter is way on the opposite side of the football field, and you feel like you'll never score a touchdown to get there. Psalm 34 is a wonderful testament of how GOD will always care for you, but there are certain verses that I want us to look at specifically. When you feel you are living a righteous life and going above and beyond, and it appears that God has gone on vacation and all you hear is silence and things are not only not improving but appear to be getting worse you can gain comfort and solace from the following verses:

Psalm 34:4 "I sought the Lord, and he heard me, and delivered me from all my fears." This is very comforting because fear comes to all of us. We need to be careful because most fear is False Evidence Appearing Real. If we succumb to this, we can become paralyzed and never live our lives. Remember John 10:10 "The thief cometh not, but for to steal, and to kill, and to destroy. I am come that they might have life and that they might have it more abundantly."

Psalm 34:6 "This poor man cried, and the Lord heard him and saved him out of all his troubles." This verse clearly states that if we will humble ourselves and cry out to God, he will save us from our troubles. Now it is important that you clearly see here that it does not say that trouble won't come and if you have lived long enough, you know trouble comes. However, God will save you and care for you.

Psalm 34:15 "The eyes of the Lord are upon the righteous, and his ears are open unto their cry." This verse states that GOD takes watchful care of his people, and his eyes and ears are attentive to their prayers.

Psalm 34:17 "The righteous cry, and the Lord heareth, and delivereth them out of all their troubles." A righteous person has a heart for GOD and tries to live in a moral and ethical way. Now you can start shouting and celebrating because this verse clearly states this person the Lord hears and delivers them out of all their troubles. Victory is right around the corner!

Psalm 34:19 "Many are the afflictions of the righteous: but the Lord delivereth him out of them all." Remember earlier when I quoted Murphy's Law (if anything can go wrong, it will). This verse allows you to take a deep breath and live your life. Life is just that its life. Suddenly you lose a loved one, your spouse announces they are leaving you, your employer states they are downsizing, and you are now out of a job, you get a negative health report from the doctor, etc. etc. This verse has been a constant comfort for me all my life because it clearly tells you that you will encounter many afflictions, but the Lord will deliver you out of them all.

I hope one of these verses has brought joy to you and lets you know everything will work out for good. Get an index card and write one of these verses and carry it in your purse or wallet for the times when you feel overwhelmed and unsure. Breathe, pray, trust GOD and Praise GOD, be thankful to GOD always and live your life.

Chapter 3

Closed Doors

What are closed doors? They are opportunities that we as humans feel are the right choices for our lives or opportunities that we currently have, but suddenly change negatively. We can make plans for our lives, but God knows what is best. The Bible says, "A man's heart deviseth his way: but the Lord directeth his steps."–Proverbs 16:9.

Closed doors happen to everyone in their lives. It can be a job that we have had for a long time and felt you would retire at this place and suddenly you are fired. It could be a home you were all set to purchase, and the seller pulled the rug from under you and sold to someone else. Closed doors and challenges come in all sizes, shapes, and forms. What we must realize is that a closed door doesn't mean it is a permanent close. It could just be temporary. However, if it isn't it is very important that we have the maturity to understand that God knows best, and he is directing our steps, so if the door closes, he has something better ahead for us. There must come a time in our spiritual lives when we must grow up and become mature believers where we don't whine and cry over every difficulty that happens in our lives.

My husband and I have a transportation company and we worked for a firm several years back that encompassed only local work within our state. However, things grew, and we branched out and did a tremendous amount of long-distance work for them where deliveries were concerned. Things were going great, and our employee driver list expanded at one point to 16. As in every business, you will have positives and negatives and eventually it became more of a burden than a joy to do the out-of-state work and so we stayed locally only. This firm had plenty of local work but hired a couple of other contractors and gave 95% of the work to them and we wound up only having work 1 day a week. When we approached them and had a meeting, the conspiracy was clear. They were looking to push us out. This hurt tremendously and caused financial issues, but this was God closing a door which boggled our minds.

When doors close on you, remember God has something greater in mind. Yes, we endured seasons of challenges, but we have come out more victorious on the other end. Keep in mind that you don't have to pay people back for the wrong they have done to you. God is your vindicator, and he will repay. We have been able to witness that firsthand with all the people that were conspiring against us that God has repaid the debt.

God Knows What He Is Doing

God is Alpha & Omega, the beginning and the end, so he knows what he is doing. God is not sitting up in the heavens rolling the dice and hoping he hits a seven or an eleven. In just six days, God created the entire world. Above and below the sea, God created every living creature. Then he created man in his own image to have dominion over everything. God knows what he is doing.

God has a purpose for your life. No matter how long it may take, just continue to trust him. Don't allow yourself to get caught up in the distractions of life. That is one of Satan's biggest tricks is to distract you from God. Trials, challenges, tests, disappointments, etc. Moses got caught in a distraction and killed an Egyptian and then ran and hid in the desert for 40 years. That did not surprise God, nor did it make him decide to use someone else to deliver the children of Israel from Pharoah.

God knew what he was doing when he led Moses to the Red Sea. All the children of Israel were panicked but God just parted the Red Sea, and they all went across safely, and Pharoah's men and their chariots drowned when God closed the Red Sea back. God knew what he was doing regarding Naaman. He was a commander in the army and had leprosy. A young girl who served advised Naaman's wife that he needed to travel to see the prophet Elisha and he would heal him. Naaman could have discounted what this young girl had to say, but he listened and went. He not only didn't meet with Elisha but still followed the orders Elisha's men told him to go wash in the dirty river Jordan seven times and then he would be cured of the leprosy, which he was. God knew what he was doing when he had Jesus wait a few extra days and not get to Lazarus immediately when he was advised how ill he was so that the miracle of Jesus raising Lazarus from the dead could take place.

God is the greatest GPS system ever. He knows precisely how he is directing your life. He is aware of all the potholes, curves, mountain terrain, flat level surfaces, peaks and valleys you will encounter. Just trust where he is leading you, because God knows what he is doing.

Failure Is Not The End It Is The Beginning

Failure is one of the greatest learning lessons ever. Too many people are afraid to step out of their comfort zone because of the fear of failure. When you fail, you learn what not to ever do again. Failure not only teaches you, but it makes us stretch and grow and this is what will bring you into your successes.

If you pull up to a gas station and park at the pump to fill up but you are so involved with the phone call, you're on that you didn't realize you picked up the diesel fuel pump and put it in your gas tank and only realize the error you've made after you have filled up your car chances are you will never be on the phone again when you need to fill up your car after the damage you caused by filling up your tank with the wrong thing the last time. Failure teaches us critical learning lessons for the future.

Thomas Edison is noted as creating the first electric lightbulb. Edison started testing designs back in 1878 with his team of researchers and finally filed for a U S patent in 1879. It is said that Edison tested over 3,000 designs for bulbs between 1878 and 1880. Thomas Edison founded the Edison Electric Light Company in 1878 in New York. Someone asked Edison about his failures, and he stated, "I have not failed. I've just found 10,000 ways that won't work."

Henry Ford filed bankruptcy twice before he could become prominent in the automobile industry. Henry Ford had a dream and a vision to invent a vehicle and, believing that he was successful in 1899, quit his job and started the Detroit Automobile Company. Unfortunately, he was not savvy enough to handle his finances and could not repay his investors and had to file bankruptcy. Undaunted by what happened several years later with his vision still in front of him and his faith, he tried again, but he didn't brand and market his vehicles properly and again could not repay his investors and had to file bankruptcy for a second time. Having these two negative marks against him did not stop him from looking to succeed and thrive. He buckled down and tried again, believing that the third time would be a charm and it was. Finally, he named the company The Ford Motor Company and never looked back.

If you never have had a test to endure, then you will never have a testimony to talk about. If you are afraid of failing, then you will never have the triumph of success.

Brokenness Induces Change

When you get to that point in life where it seems like everything you have tried didn't work, you feel lost. You are downhearted; you feel completely empty, you just don't know whether you are going to survive. This is when you feel broken. You are not alone. This happens to all of us in our lives. Sometimes we reach this point because of trials, challenges, tests taking place in our lives. However, sometimes we bring this upon ourselves.

This happened to King David in the Bible. God blessed him abundantly, and he thought he deserved anything and everything and he should have everything he set his eyes on that he desired. WRONG! This is when you become prideful, and any shred of humility has exited you.

David, with all his wives and concubines, fell in love with a woman named Bathsheba. This was not the main issue. Bathsheba was married to a man named Uriah. David became so obsessed to have Bathsheba that he had her husband Uriah killed and then married Bathsheba and slept with her and she became pregnant. It sorely displeased God with what David had done that as a punishment the baby died. Once David repented and got back in God's graces, Bathsheba became pregnant again and gave birth to Solomon.

Now everybody has their own tale of woe, but did you bring it on yourself? Whether you did or you didn't there will come a time in your life when you feel brokenness. This is when you put your shoulders back and realize that something good is on the way. Remember, whatever goes down must come back up again. Think about a hot-air balloon. It goes up and down, taking people on some of the most breathtaking air rides ever.

Now, if you have been mishandling things in your life, then it is important to repent and get back on track. The same way that God restored David after he repented and completed his punishment, God will do the same for you. If you have been mishandling your relationships, finances, health or others, you can change. If you have been treating your spouse or family members or friends wrong and now no one wants to have anything to do with you, that means you have encountered brokenness. Repent, pray, and start treating them in the same way you would want to be treated. If you have been frivolous with money and now are in a financial situation, change the way you manage your finances and give to others. That is the fastest way to reap a harvest is by giving. Remember that your body is the temple of the Lord, where the Holy Spirit lives. If you are filling it with a host of unhealthy things and now when you go to the doctor, the medical report is not good, you are in a broken state. You now must make changes that will improve your quality of life. There is also the possibility that the career path you chose and believed you would retire from has cut you and you're lost. You believe you are too old to go back to school to learn a new trade. This, of course, is unfair, but maybe it is a closed door. You were an ideal employee, and you feel you deserve better, but keep in mind the rain falls on the just and the unjust. God has something greater ahead waiting for you. Remember, God's word, you can do all things through Christ that strengthens you.

Chapter 4

The Seasons Of Life

"To everything, there is a season, and a time to every purpose under the heaven: a time to be born, and a time to die; a time to plant, and a time to pluck up that which is planted; A time to kill, and a time to heal; a time to break down, and a time to build up; A time to weep, and a time to laugh; a time to mourn, and a time to dance; A time to cast away stones, and a time to gather stones together; a time to embrace, and a time to refrain from embracing; A time to get, and a time to lose; a time to keep, and a time to cast away; A time to rend, and a time to sew; a time to keep silence, and a time to speak; A time to love, and a time to hate; a time of war and a time of peace." -Ecclesiastes 3:1-8.

The same way that we have Winter, Spring, Summer, & Fall is the same way that we all have seasons in our lives where we encounter highs and lows. Just like in spring, some things will go well and be ready for harvest and some things may need more time. That doesn't mean we give up on our dreams and pursuits we just must persevere. Sometimes in life we must do a lot of weeding and cutting. Ants are insects we can learn a lot from. Ants never quit. When they are on the trail for food, they don't let any obstacle stand in their way. They just don't stand there shaking their heads in disbelief. They don't give up on their goal.

They don't feel sorry for themselves and decide that success isn't for them. They confront their obstacles and walk around it, over it, though it or under it, until they achieve their desired outcome. We all will have fall seasons in our lives as well. Fall is also stressful sometimes. Children are returning to school, more traffic on the roadways because the schools have re-opened. With children returning to school, then all their school activities such as football, music class, ballet, etc. come back and take even more of a dent out of our daily grinds. Our employers are looking for strong closing 3rd quarter tax numbers before the 4th quarter starts. This is when we need to pace ourselves and connect closer to God to renew our strength every day. "But they that wait upon the Lord shall renew their strength; they shall mount up with wings as eagles; they shall run, and not be weary, and they shall walk, and not faint."–Isaiah 40:31. When the wintry weather comes around and there are cold rainy days and the snows have descended upon us and we revert to eastern standard time, for some of us, things can become a little depressing. One great pick me up is the Christmas lights on people's homes and stores. Sometimes in everyone's life when things go wrong and not according to plan it is painful. Unfortunately, I can almost guarantee that there will be disappointments and let-downs, making certain periods of your life seem like Winter. However, statements like, "Life is always hard and disappointing", "I can never get ahead where things go my way" and "I'm always stressed" can be extremely damaging and depressing after a while, making our low periods seem longer and sometimes actually last longer. Understand that tough times always end, things get better, and Summer is coming!

Yes, the rain falls on the just & the unjust, but as a believer, remember, life is what you make it. Sure, there will be highs and lows, but try changing your thought pattern. Say things like, "I have an inbuilt optimism and know that the lean times won't last forever. Everything and everybody prospers me." Look at the glass as if it is half full and not half empty.

Blessings Disguised As Burdens

All of us, in life, encounter some arduous times. We stumble into trials, chaos, testing periods, challenges that look like they will never go away and are higher than Mount Everest's peak. Those of us that are believers feel we should never have to deal with such things. We think we do our best; we live a godly life, so why is this happening? Sometimes your burdens are blessings in disguise.

These tests, trials, burdens that you go through that you believe are going to sink you are the preparation for you to walk into the abundant blessings God has for you. God wants the best for you. He said it in his word; however, you must be ready to step into it. God does not want you to fail and if he gives you something that you are not ready for, that is exactly what will happen... you will FAIL. God wants to make sure that you are equipped for the blessing so that once you step into it, you stay in it and just keep rising higher and higher instead of sinking down into the sand.

Most of you are aware of the Bible story of Joseph. In the Bible Joseph was told in a dream that he was going to be a high-ranking official but what he didn't know is all the burdens he would have to endure and how long it would take to reach that pinnacle and be living that dream. His brothers threw him in a pit, and he was picked up by a caravan and taken to Pharoah. They placed him in jail because Pharoah's wife lied and said he tried to be intimate with her when he didn't. One of the people in jail became friends with Joseph and promised to speak with Pharoah about releasing him when he was released but he forgot, and Joseph remained in jail until Pharoah had a disturbing dream and since God had blessed Joseph to interpret dreams, he was called by Pharoah, and he interpreted the dream and finally he was released, and Pharoah made Joseph second in command behind him. From the time that Joseph's brothers threw him into the pit until Pharoah made him second in command under him was thirteen years.

Nowadays we get what they call alerts to our phones. Especially if it is an AMBER alert. What is an amber alert? The AMBER Alert System began in 1996 when Dallas-Fort Worth broadcasters teamed with local police to develop an early warning system to help find abducted children. AMBER stands for America's Missing: Broadcast Emergency Response and was created as a legacy to 9-year-old

Amber Hagerman, who was kidnapped while riding her bicycle in Arlington, TX, and then brutally murdered. Other states and communities soon set up their own AMBER plans, as we adopted the idea across the nation. Well, God's alerts are blessings disguised as burdens. Every time you encounter a challenging situation, it is a test that God is putting you through to determine if you are ready to receive the blessing you have been asking about. Now, since none of us like to be away from our blanket like the one Linus had in the Peanuts cartoon and we always want to be comfortable, God will not allow that to happen. If you want great things, you must take substantial risks and go through many tests and struggles. The more you ask for and the bigger your dreams, then just strap yourself in because it is going to be a long ride. If Jesus had to endure the cross, what makes us believe we are above reproach? Don't pray away all the unpleasant things that happen in your life and the burdens you must bear because they are the things that are going to elevate you to the blessing you have been asking God for.

God's Grace

God gives us grace every day to accomplish what we need to execute. You want to pray and ask God for his grace daily. God's grace blesses your life. God does not give us grace days, weeks, months, or years in advance. Every 24 hours, God gives us grace for the day.

During World War II, there was a young woman named Corrie Ten Boom who worked with her father, sister, and family members to assist several Jews to escape the Nazis from the Holocaust during World War II by hiding them in her home. Ultimately, she and her family were captured and placed in prison. While there, she witnessed many cruel acts, physical violence, and injuries. Unfortunately, she even witnessed the deaths of her sister and father. With a miracle turn of events, they released Corrie.

Someone asked Corrie how she could live through those awful events and not carry malice and unforgiveness in her heart for the people who murdered her father and sister. Corrie spoke about how when she was a small child, her father always took her on train rides. She recounted how her father would never give her the train ticket until he saw the train pulling into the station. When the train arrived that was when her father handed her the ticket and they both stepped onboard. Corrie stated, "The reason you can't fathom how I could forgive the person who killed my family, how I could not be filled with bitterness and hatred, is because just like my father and our train tickets, God doesn't give us the grace we need until we're about to step onboard. But if you were to ever go through something like I went through, I can assure you God's grace will be there to help you make it through the dark valleys and keep your head held high and your heart filled with love."

Bible Verses on Grace:

"And he said unto me, My grace is sufficient for thee: for my strength is made perfect in weakness. Most gladly, therefore, will I rather glory in my infirmities, that the power of Christ may rest upon me." –2 Corinthians 12:9.

"For by grace are ye saved through faith; and that not of yourselves: it is the gift of God." –Ephesians 2:8

"But he giveth more grace. Wherefore he saith, God resisteth the proud, but giveth grace unto the humble." –James 4:6

"But by the grace of God, I am what I am: and his grace which was bestowed upon me was not in vain, but I laboured more abundantly than they all: yet not I, but the grace of God which was with me." -1 Corinthians 15:10

"And of his fulness have all we received, and grace for grace." –John 1:16

"For the grace of God that bringeth salvation hath appeared to all men." –Titus 2:11

"Being justified freely by his grace through the redemption that is in Christ Jesus." –Romans 3:24

"Thou, therefore, my son, be strong in the grace that is in Christ Jesus." –2 Timothy 2:1

When you are looking to overcome, remember that God is the conductor and has a ticket for you and will give it to you at the appropriate time. God will also give you the grace you need to accomplish whatever you need to do!

Breathe

"And the Lord God formed man of the dust of the ground and breathed into his nostrils the breath of life; and man became a living soul." –Genesis 2:7

"By the word of the Lord, were the heavens made; and all the host of them by the breath of his mouth." –Psalm 33:6

No matter what is going on around you or whatever is surrounding, you just breathe. This is how existence started by God breathing the breath of life in Adam. God has designs on what he wants each of us to accomplish in life and he is with you every step of the way. If you have the breath of life, that means that God is not done with you. Every day that we wake up, that means that God has given us the breath of life for one more time. We have been given another 86,400 seconds if we make it through the day to breathe. When you have breath, that means that God still has plans for your life because when you stop breathing and you die, that means he is done with you.

Many people miss the mark by getting caught up with distractions. Remember, I said earlier that Satan puts distractions in our path to prevent us from doing the assignments that God assigned to us. When we don't complete our assignments, then God no longer has use for us and we perish. I've heard it said that the wealthiest place in the world is the cemeteries because of all the assignments God had for us we never executed. Whether that was because of fear or anything else, we didn't complete them. Like Steve Harvey says, you must JUMP or else you will never attain the greatness that God sent his son Jesus to die for you. The same way that God has plans for you is the same way that Satan has plans to stop you from reaching your goals and moving into that life of abundance that Jesus died to give you. "The thief cometh not, but for to steal, and to kill, and to destroy I am come that they might have life, and that they might have it more abundantly."–John 10:10. "Now unto him that is able to do exceeding abundantly above all that we ask or think, according to the power that worketh in us," -Ephesians 3:20.

For every day that you live, God has his plan for your life and Satan has one as well. God's plan is to take you step by step into that good life that Jesus died for you to have, and Satan's plan is to distract you, so you never get there. If you have ever wondered why, you had a great night's sleep, but as soon as you wake up, your mind is bombarded with negative thoughts and feelings, and you can't shake them. That is Satan and his army trying to get you going in a downward spiral before you even get out of bed. It is very important that you fight off the negative and reach for the positive. Therefore, memorizing Bible verses are so important so when the attack comes you can retaliate immediately before Satan gets an upper hand. When thoughts tell you that you can't accomplish your goals, you fight back with, "I can do all things through Christ which strengthens me."–Philippians 4:13. When other thoughts tell you that health issue that you have that runs in your family or the addiction that you have been trying to beat you never will and you will succumb to it you retaliate back and say, "No weapon that is formed against thee shall prosper; and every tongue that shall rise against thee in judgment thou shalt condemn. This is the heritage of the servants of the Lord, and their righteousness is of me, saith the Lord."–Isaiah 54:17.

Time is moving swiftly, and life is short, so you need to be steadfast and strive to accomplish the assignment that God set for you when he created you. Our birth date and death date have already been determined and assigned by God, so it is important that we stay diligent and focus on our goals and assignment from God. We cannot afford distractions of any type. When they come and they will in many forms just breathe. Breathing is one of the first things they teach you in yoga. Satan has an arsenal of weapons to throw at us. On those days, that is when you think this is Murphy's Law, (if anything can go wrong, it will). Your child is behaving unruly for the day, when the car gets a flat tire, when you are cooking dinner and it burns, when your dog refuses to go in the backyard and relieve himself, your husband refuses to take out the garbage, your laptop freezes, and you were in the middle of working on your proposal for work. STOP & BREATHE. These are the distractions Satan sends.

Pray, speak of God's goodness and the gratitude you feel for all he has done in your life and BREATHE. Remember, this too shall pass and to everything, there is a season.

Chapter 5

God Uses Our Deepest Pain To Be The Launching Pad Of Our Future

I realize that at first glance, the title of this section may appear to be surreal. Then once you give it a brief thought, you think if God only wants the best for us all, then why would he do this? Then, for those of you that are analytical, you will spend hours or even days trying to decipher why that is. I am going to sum this up simply for you. God speaks to us all in a soft whisper. He also tries to nudge us in the correct direction, but we must be open to feeling his presence and when we are constantly distracted with the wrong things, he will allow the choices we have made because he gave us all free will to take place.

This is clear from the beginning of time in the Bible book of Genesis with Adam & Eve. They both made a choice to listen to the serpent and that disastrous choice gave Satan control of the world until Jesus came and took control back. "The thief cometh not, but for to steal, and to kill, and to destroy. I am come that they might have life, and that they might have it more abundantly."–John 10:10.

When we have sunk to our lowest lows, that is when we cry out to God more than ever. Sure, there will be times when we didn't bring the trouble to ourselves just like Job in the Bible, however a lot of the times our deepest pain is brought on ourselves for the poor choices we make. When we are in these lackluster situations, that is when God can hold us and get us back on track to the abundant life, he desires for all of us.

There is a beautiful story that I read many years ago about molding and shaping that I am going to include here for you to read. This story will bring a lot of light and meaning to what I am saying. Stay open & pliable so God can mold you into the jewel he desires you to become.

The Potter's Wheel–The Teacup

The story is told of a couple who went to England to celebrate their 25th wedding anniversary and shopped at a beautiful antique store. They both liked antiques and pottery, and especially teacups, and so spotting an exceptional cup, they asked, "May we see that? We've never seen a cup quite so beautiful."

As the lady handed it to them, suddenly the teacup spoke. "You don't understand." It said, "I have not always been a teacup. There was a time when I was just a lump of red clay. My master took me and rolled me, pounded and patted me over and over and I yelled out, don't do that. I don't like it!" "Let me alone," but he only smiled, and gently said; "Not yet!!" "Then, WHAM! I was placed on a spinning wheel and suddenly I was spun around and around and around." "Stop it! I'm getting so dizzy!" "I'm going to be sick!" I screamed.

But the master only nodded and said, quietly; 'Not yet.'

He spun me and poked and prodded and bent me out of shape to suit himself and then... he put me in the oven. I never felt such heat. I yelled and knocked and pounded at the door.

"Help! Get me out of here!" 'Not yet.' When I thought I couldn't bear it another minute, the door opened. He carefully took me out and put me on the shelf, and I began to cool.

Oh, that felt so good! "Ah, this is much better," I thought. But after I cooled, he picked me up, and he brushed and painted me all over. The fumes were horrible. "Oh, please, Stop it! Stop it!" I cried. He only shook his head and said. "Not yet..."

Then suddenly he put me back into the oven. Only it was not like the first time. This time it was twice as hot, and I just knew I would suffocate. I begged... I pleaded... I screamed... I cried... I was convinced I would never make it. I was ready to give up and just then the door opened, and he took me out and again placed me on the shelf, where I cooled and waited and waited, wondering "What's he going to do to me next?"

An hour later, he handed me a mirror and said, "Look at yourself."

And I did... I said, "That's not me, that couldn't be me. It's beautiful. I'm beautiful!"

Quietly he spoke: "I want you to remember, then," he said, "I know it hurt to be rolled and pounded and patted, but had I just left you alone, you'd have dried up. I know it made you dizzy to spin around on the wheel, but if I had stopped, you would have crumbled."

"I know it hurt, and it was hot and disagreeable in the oven, but if I hadn't put you there, you would have cracked. I know the fumes were bad when I brushed and painted you all over, but if I hadn't done that, you never would have hardened. You would not have had any color in your life."

"And if I hadn't put you back in that second oven, you wouldn't have survived for long because the hardness would not have held. Now you are a finished product. Now you are what I had in mind when I first began with you."

Author Unknown

No Matter What Curve Balls Come At You Just Keep Swinging

In the sport MLB, the overall view from hitters is that the curveball is the toughest pitch to hit. There are books and DVDs about this subject and the mechanics of how to have success. I want us to look at three mechanics and compare them to the life of a believer.

In an article titled "Short To The Ball" written by Chris O' Leary, he stated that Short to the Ball, as it's generally used, means taking the hands DIRECTLY to the ball. We as believers need to do the same thing, especially when we are in the situation where the rain falls on the just and the unjust. We need to go directly to God and pray and talk with him. God is a miracle working God and he can fix things in the blink of an eye. Sometimes it takes longer, and that is when there are issues, he is trying to work on where we are concerned. Just because it is not an instant fix, don't think that God won't fix the situation. Sure, it is fine to call friends and get their opinion of what to do, but we need to go Short to the ball and go to the mainline first, which is God.

There was a blog article written by a firm called "FirstPitch" that is in Maple Plain Minnesota that discussed the mechanics of "No Drifting or Dropping." The article stated that, "You can't let your eyes drift or drop when trying to hit a curveball. You must stay disciplined to ensure a smart swing. If your eyes drift or drop, you will register the pitch to be moving much faster than it is actually traveling. This will cause you to miss most pitches but is especially detrimental when hitting a curveball." This is a critical part of the life of a believer in God. You cannot allow the naysayers to take you off the path of believing and trusting God. You must remain convicted and committed. This life that God has given us is a journey. How you handle the journey is just as important as the destination.

In that same article from "FirstPitch" they discussed another mechanic for hitting a curveball which is called "Always On Top." They described this is, "When hitting a curveball, you always want to get on top. This means keeping the barrel of your bat up and always keeping your eyes above the pitch. This forces you to avoid dropping the barrel in too soon or being too long during the swing." Praise & Worship is very important in your walk with God. When you are constantly giving God the accolades, he deserves that makes him work even more diligently on the issues in your life. When you praise and thank him in advance before the victory, you are showing him you have complete faith and trust in him. When the children of Israel had crossed over the Red Sea and were on the other side and Pharoah's men & chariots were drowned in the sea, they pulled out their tambourines and sang praises and worshipped God. This, of course, pleased God, but how much sweeter would it have been if they were Always On Top and did this before they stepped into the victory?

When You Feel Like You're Drowning

We have all at some time or another felt like we were drowning. It happens when we are facing trials, tests, and challenges that seem to get stronger and larger instead of disappearing. This is when we feel like we are in a constant winter season. This is when we are questioning ourselves about what I must do to see light at the end of the tunnel. These are the times when we are craving for a manifestation. This is when we believe that we have reached the end of our rope. The problems are too big, too tall, too smelly for you to overcome. This, however, is when God's grace kicks in.

"When you feel like you're drowning in life, don't worry—your lifeguard walks on water."–Anonymous

Life is a journey, and, in all journeys, you have highs and lows. There are some straight paths and some crooked paths. There will be some smooth and bumpy roads. There are some areas that are well lit and some that are completely dark. You will have peaks and valleys, as well as ebb and flow. You will encounter mountains to climb as well as straight paths to walk.

Life can be beautiful and messy at the same time. You must make a choice if you are just going to lie down and allow the dust to cover you and eventually, with weather conditions, just disintegrate and die. Disintegrate - to undergo a change in composition. https://www.merriam-webster.com/dictionary/disintegrate

Your other choice is simply just to pick yourself up, dust yourself off, and start all over again and just keep moving forward. Or, as the phrase says, "cowboy up." The phrase cowboy up it means when things are getting tough you have to get back up, dust yourself off and keep trying. - https://www.urbandictionary.com/define.php?term=cowboy%20up.

When you feel like you're drowning, remember that God is with you, and he is an ever-present help in times of trouble. This is what the Bible tells us, "God is our refuge and strength, a very present help in trouble."–Psalm 46;1. There is no trouble that we bring on ourselves or that comes to us that God cannot fix and make disappear. A prime example of this would be the story of Peter walking on water coming to Jesus and then he allowed doubt to creep into his head, and he immediately started to drown, and Jesus extended his hand and saved him.

"And straightway Jesus constrained his disciples to get into a ship, and to go before him unto the other side, while he sent the multitudes away. And when he had sent the multitudes away, he went up into a mountain apart to pray and when the evening was come, he was there alone. But the ship was now in the midst of the sea, tossed with waves: for the wind was contrary. And in the fourth watch of the night Jesus went unto them, walking on the sea. And when the disciples saw him walking on the sea, they were troubled, saying, it is a spirit; and they cried out for fear. But straightway Jesus spake unto them, saying, be of good cheer; it is I; be not afraid. And Peter answered him and said, Lord, if it be thou, bid me come unto thee on the water. And he said, Come. And when Peter was come down out of the ship, he walked on the water, to go to Jesus. But when he saw the wind boisterous, he was afraid; and beginning to sink, he cried, saying, Lord, save me. And immediately Jesus stretched forth his hand, and caught him, and said unto him, O thou of little faith, wherefore didst thou doubt? And when they were come into the ship, the wind ceased. Then they that were in the ship came and worshipped him, saying, Of a truth thou art the Son of God." - Matthew 14:22-33.

When you feel like you're drowning remember that Jesus is your floatation device, and he will pull you back up and stabilize your life.

God Is Never Surprised

Often, we are surprised by events that happen in our lives. When these things happen, we start to scramble and try to figure out how we are going to fix things ourselves. This is our first mistake because we are not capable of doing anything on our own. We must seek God for help in all areas of our lives.

God, because he is Alpha & Omega, is never surprised with anything that happens. It says so in his word the Bible:

"I am the Lord: that is my name: and my glory will I not give to another, neither my praise to graven images. Behold, the former things are come to pass, and new things do I declare: before they spring forth I tell you of them." -Isaiah 42:8-9.

"For if our heart condemn us, God is greater than our heart, and knoweth all things." –1 John 3:20.

"And they prayed, and said, Thou, Lord, which knowest the hearts of all men, shew whether of these two thou hast chosen." –Acts 1:24

"The eyes of the Lord are in every place, beholding the evil and the good." –Proverbs 15:3

"But the very hairs of your head are all numbered." –Matthew 10:30

It does not surprise God about where you are right now. If things are bad, he is not taken off guard. He is not shocked about what has happened to you. God knows every situation we come into better than we can ever understand it. It did not surprise God when Peter cut off a man's ear. He wasn't when Jonah was swallowed by a whale. When Noah had to build an ark. He wasn't when Adam and Eve bit into the fruit. We all give ourselves much more credit than we should. We think we know exactly how our lives should progress and end up. We make our plans, but don't realize that God's thoughts are higher than ours. He has placed a gift or gifts inside of us and knows exactly what our purpose in life is. "Having then gifts differing according to the grace that is given to us, whether prophecy, let us prophesy according to the proportion of faith; Or ministry, let us wait on our ministering: or he that teacheth, on teaching; Or he that exhorteth, on exhortation: he that giveth, let him do it with simplicity; he that ruleth, with diligence; he that sheweth mercy, with cheerfulness." –Romans 12:6-8.

I watched a movie a while ago called "The Right Girl", It is a Hallmark Movie. I love Hallmark movies. The essence of the movie had to do with a young woman who lost her father and started down a selfish, obnoxious path with her dealings with people since she was wealthy. Her mother arranged with their attorney to notify her that both the mother and she had lost all their money, reckless spending and poor investments and would have to survive. She had to get a job that she never had and wound up working two jobs at one point. She had to share an apartment with her mother, use a loaner car from a friend which was a far cry from the corvette she was driving at the beginning of the movie. She eventually humbled herself and became a giving, caring, considerate, loving person, which is the person her mother knew was inside of her. Eventually, her mother told her the truth and notified her that all her money was there and placed it all back in her bank accounts. She thanked her mother for doing what she did because that changed her life.

God is never surprised, sometimes there are lessons that we have to learn the hard way, which is what will bless our lives exponentially.

Chapter 6

You Are Built To Withstand

As much as Satan tries to tell you that you are not good enough, strong enough, your heavenly father tells you that you are built to withstand. "Watch, stand fast in the faith, be brave, be strong." 1 Corinthians 16:13. "Therefore take up the whole armor of God, that you may be able to withstand in the evil day, and having done all, to stand." –Ephesians 6:13.

Most people have heard of the biblical story of David & Goliath. David loved God. He was a small shepherd boy and the youngest of eight sons of his father, Jesse. His brothers and his father looked down upon David. His brothers were in the army, and they liked to belittle him. One day, his father asked him to take lunch to his brothers, and he came upon Goliath. There were two tribes, the Philistines and the Israelites, who were planning to war against each other and Goliath, who was a mammoth man in height and size, kept taunting the Israelites to send a man to fight him. They stated that whatever tribe won, they would control the other. David realized this and offered to fight Goliath. King Saul wanted no part of this because of how small David was, but eventually agreed after David demanded to fight Goliath. King Saul even offered David his armor before going into battle, but David rejected it after he tried it on, and it just weighed him down. So, King Saul told David, "Go, and the Lord be with you!"

Goliath, when he saw David, made fun of him and declared it would be simple work killing David. Upon traveling to the showdown spot where the two men would meet, David found five smooth stones and placed them in his shepherd's bag. When David approached Goliath, he said, "You come to me with a sword, with a spear, and with a javelin. But I come to you in the name of the Lord of hosts, the God of the armies of Israel, whom you have defied. This day, the Lord will deliver you into my hand, and I will strike you and take your head from you. And this day I will give the carcasses of the camp of the Philistines to the birds of the air and the wild beasts of the earth, that all the earth may know that there is a God in Israel. Then all this assembly shall know that the Lord does not save with sword and spear; for the battle is the Lord's, and He will give you into our hands."–1 Samuel 17:45-47.

David took one of his smooth stones and swung it at Goliath and he fell face down. Then David took Goliath's own sword and cut off his head and killed him instantly. And so, David killed Goliath and won the victory for the Israelites, which kept them from becoming slaves to the Philistines.

David carried five smooth stones with him, but he only needed one to knock Goliath down and then used his sword to finish him. You and God are a majority. When God created you, he put in you all the weapons and strength you would need to stand strong and always withstand. Even though you are a believer, that doesn't mean strong winds won't come at you. It also doesn't mean that piles of snow won't be dumped on you or earth-shattering events like how earthquakes rattle things, but you must stand strong in your mind and remember that even though the rain falls on the just and the unjust you were built to withstand.

A Lie Only Runs Until It Is Taken Over By the Truth

There is an old saying, "tell the truth and shame the devil." The saying originated from a preacher. They recorded this in his book, ""Twenty-Seven Sermons," published in 1555. This saying became more popular because of Shakespeare, who used the saying in his play, "Henry IV. Part I, performed in 1597. There is another saying from the Bible which states, "therefore whatever you have spoken in the dark will be heard in the light, and what you have spoken in the ear in inner rooms will be proclaimed on the housetops."–Luke 12:3.

There is a Chengyu story in China that is over 2000 years old. It is a story about a man who pretended to be a musician who played in an ensemble for a royal family. His name was Nan Guo. The story states that there was a king who really enjoyed listening to music, so an ensemble was created to play for the king. Nan Guo wanted so much to be a part of this ensemble, but he could not play any instrument. However, he was wealthy and offered money to become a part of the ensemble. The maestro gave him a flute, and he joined the ensemble and pretended to play the flute. He would move his fingers around and everybody thought he was for real. He was able to keep this charade up for several years. Eventually, the king retired, and the prince took over. To Nao Guo's shock the prince preferred for people to play individually for him and not as an ensemble so when he was called in to play the ruse was over and he had to come clean and tell the truth that he could not play the instrument. Once the truth was revealed, Nao Guo was so embarrassed that he just disappeared and was never heard from again.

This is what eventually will happen to Satan because when God comes back to take his world back Satan's multitude of lies will be exposed and the righteous and the believers who stood tall and firm and kept their faith, trust, belief, and eyes on God will be crowned and remain with God for all eternity.

Perseverance

The definition of perseverance says the quality that allows someone to continue trying to do something even though it is difficult. - http://www.merriam-webster.com/

If we are to enjoy the good things in life that GOD wants for us, we all must learn how to persevere. Nothing good in life comes without endurance and hard work. Does God really want us to enjoy the good things in life and live abundantly? You better believe he does because he says it in his word. We all must stay grounded and persevere, because that is the only option. The only other thing is to stop trying, stop reaching and when we default to this, then we are not moving forward, and God cannot bless you when you are stagnant.

"I'm convinced that about half of what separates the successful entrepreneurs from the non-successful ones is pure perseverance." – Steve Jobs (1955-2011).

"Genius is divine perseverance. Genius, I cannot claim nor even extra brightness but perseverance all can have." Woodrow Wilson.

"To persevere in one's duty and be silent is the best answer to calumny." - George Washington

"If you are going through hell, keep going." - Winston S. Churchill

"It doesn't matter how slowly you go as long as you don't stop." - Confucius

"It always seems impossible until it's done." - Nelson Mandela

"Many of life's failures are people who did not realize how close they were to success when they gave up." - Thomas A. Edison

"I am a slow walker, but I never walk back." - Abraham Lincoln

"Never confuse a single defeat with a final defeat." - F. Scott Fitzgerald

"If you fell down yesterday, stand up today." - H. G. Wells

"Every strike brings me closer to the next home run." - Babe Ruth

"When things go wrong, don't go with them." - Elvis Presley

"When you get to the end of your rope. Tie a knot and hang on." - Franklin D. Roosevelt

"Once you learn to quit, it becomes a habit". - Vince Lombardi Jr.

"Dreams become reality through faith and perseverance." - K D Hanes

"Get on top of the obstacles and they become vantage points." - Tom Althouse

"I've often said a man's character is not judged after he celebrates a victory, but what he does when his back is against the wall. So no matter how great the setback, how severe the failure, you never give up." - John Cena

"Life is not easy for any of us. But what of that? We must have perseverance and, above all, confidence in ourselves. We must believe that we are gifted for something, and that this thing, at whatever cost, must be attained"–Marie Curie.

"Who is the wise man? He who sees what's going to be born." - King Solomon

One of the greatest examples of perseverance is the famous artist, Vincent Van Gogh. He "was a Dutch Post-Impressionist painter who posthumously became one of the most famous and influential figures in Western art history. In a decade, he created about 2,100 artworks, including around 860 oil paintings, most of which date from the last two years of his life. They include landscapes, still lifes, portraits, and self-portraits, and are characterised by bold colours and dramatic, impulsive and expressive brushwork that contributed to the foundations of modern art." - https://en.wikipedia.org/wiki/Vincent_van_Gogh

Image having such a strong passion and the perseverance to match it that a person creates over 2,100 works of art. Some say that to determine what is your purpose and passion is to discover what you love to do the most and that takes the least amount of time to execute. Also include in that equation what it is that you would be willing to do for hours on end and never get paid for doing.

God took six days to create the world and rested on the seventh. He knew exactly what he wanted to do and so no matter how long it took each day he persevered to finish what was needed each day so that he would be finished by the sixth day so he could rest on the seventh once he was pleased with what he had done. The Bible says that God knew you before you were formed in your mother's womb, and he approved of you and considers you a masterpiece. Don't doubt what God says about you. Whatever assignment he has given you, just persevere. He is right by your side. Some days may look like you are all alone in the ocean without a paddle, but God is always near and constantly directing your steps. He did not promise that just because you are a believer and try to do as close to good as possible that things would go smooth. Just remember the same way he was with the three Hebrew teenagers in the fiery furnace he is with you as well. Yes, the rain falls on the just and the unjust, but where the unjust gets a tsunami, the just get a thunderstorm.

Endure With Patience

Endurance means the ability to do something difficult for a long time, the ability to deal with pain or suffering that continues for a long time; the quality of continuing for a long time. https://www.britannica.com/dictionary/endurance

Patience means the capacity, habit, or fact of being patient, able to remain calm and not become annoyed when waiting for a long time or when dealing with problems or difficult people; done in a careful way over a long period of time without hurrying. https://www.merriam-webster.com/dictionary/patience

We have become a fast-paced society. We have no patience or time for anything! Once electricity was created, the world was on the move. We could cook food in ovens and stoves, but that was not fast enough, so the microwave was invented. Did you know that in foreign countries like Italy, they prefer not to use microwaves? Italians in Italy have a different pace of life than Americans in America. They are not in such a big hurry that they force their meals into tiny microseconds. They enjoy eating. The act of coming together to enjoy a meal is very important to them. We had dialed up internet and that became obsolete with lightning high speed internet.

Think about how complex the human body and life on earth are. We have cells, organs, organ systems, homeostasis mechanisms, a highly functional brain and more. They are so complex and so many building blocks are required for them to function, yet they do. Even GOD took six days to create the earth. "And God saw everything that he had made and behold, it was very good. And the evening and the morning were the sixth day." -Genesis 1:31

We must learn to endure and be patient! Not everything can be at lightning speed:

A mother carries a child for nine months unless it is premature

The children of Israel had to endure 40 years in the wilderness

A farmer must be patient when he plants his seeds waiting for a harvest

If they catch you speeding, you must endure and wait patiently for the officer to either give you a warning and let you go or even longer if he writes you a ticket

BIBLE VERSES ON ENDURANCE

"And not only so, but we glory in tribulations also: knowing that tribulation worketh patience." -Romans 5:3

"Blessed is the man that endureth temptation: for when he is tried, he shall receive the crown of life, which the Lord hath promised to them that love him." -James 1:12

"But let patience have her perfect work, that ye may be perfect and entire, wanting nothing." -James 1:4

BIBLE VERSES ON PATIENCE

"And let us not be weary in well doing for in due season we shall reap, if we faint not." -Galatians 6:9

"But they that wait upon the LORD shall renew [their] strength; they shall mount up with wings as eagles; they shall run and not be weary; [and] they shall walk, and not faint." -Isiah 40:31

"Rest in the LORD and wait patiently for him: fret not thyself because of him who prospereth in his way, because of the man who bringeth wicked devices to pass." -Psalm 37:7

Think about the patience and endurance God has had with all of us. When he created this world, he wasn't expecting we would make the poor choices that we have made. He could have destroyed all of us many times over, just like he did when he asked Noah to build the ark. However, with his love, goodness, patience, and endurance, it is over 2,000 years and Jesus has not come back yet.

QUOTES ON ENDURANCE

"No pain that we suffer, no trial that we experience is wasted. It ministers to our education, to the development of such qualities as patience, faith, fortitude and humility. All that we suffer and all that we endure, especially when we endure it patiently, builds up our characters, purifies our hearts, expand our souls, and makes us more tender and charitable, more worthy to be called the children of God... and it is through sorrow and suffering, toil and tribulation, that we gain the education that we come here to acquire and which will make us more like our Father and Mother in heaven."

—— Orson F. Whitney

"All through my life, I have been tested. My will has been tested, my courage has been tested, my strength has been tested. Now my patience and endurance are being tested." —— Muhammad Ali

"And St. Francis said: 'My dear son, be patient, because the weaknesses of the body are given to us in this world by God for the salvation of the soul. So they are of great merit when they are borne patiently." —— Francis of Assisi

QUOTES ON PATIENCE

"He that can have patience can have what he will." —— Benjamin Franklin

"Patience is bitter, but its fruit is sweet." —— Aristotle

"Toleration is the greatest gift of the mind; it requires the same effort of the brain that it takes to balance oneself on a bicycle." —— Helen Keller

"It is easier to find men who will volunteer to die, than to find those who are willing to endure pain with patience." - Julius Caesar

"Patience serves as a protection against wrongs as clothes do against cold. For if you put on more clothes as the cold increases, it will have no power to hurt you. So in like manner you must grow in patience when you meet with great wrongs, and they." - Leonardo da Vinci.

When the rain falls on the just and the unjust when it is all over the just see a rainbow in the sky.

Chapter 7

Keep A Vision Of Victory

Your thought life is very important so you must guard that extraordinarily because what you think is what will determine your future and if you want to live a victorious one, you must guard your thoughts and keep a vision of victory.

It is of the utmost importance to have a vision for your life. For young children, they can grasp this right away when they think about Tinker Bell from the story of Peter Pan. In the movie Peter Pan says the following, ""All it takes is faith and trust... Oh! And something I forgot: Dust. Just a little bit of pixie dust." I want you to channel your vision of victory like pixie dust. This magical substance pixie dust in the movie grants the ability of flight. In life, we all want to fly high victoriously, and so you need to cultivate that vision of victory for your life.

Now it is also critical that once you have this vision of victory for your life that you realize it is not just going to drop in your lap. You must work for it. The Bible says, "He that tilleth his land shall be satisfied with bread: but he that followeth vain persons is void of understanding." –Proverbs 12:11. For example you cannot just create a vison board and then just lie on your back daydreaming and waiting for things to happen. You have a part and God has a part in the victorious life he has planned for you.

Keep your faith and trust in God and keep that vison of victory for your life while you work at obtaining the abundant life that God says he has for you and no matter how much rain falls in your life you will be triumphant and thrive.

Perspective

The definition of perspective is the capacity to view things in their true relations or relative importance. - https://www.merriam-webster.com/dictionary/perspective

Your perspective plays a critical role in your daily life. If you are looking at life in a negative connotation, you will make poor choices which will lead you away from God and down a destructive, deadly path. You must learn to look at the glass half full and not half empty. You must see closed doors as a positive and not a negative in your life. Yes, the rain falls on the just and the unjust, but the just have protective rain gear which is God.

Your perspective can either hold you hostage and keep you tangled up, or it can have you living a life of freedom that is light and breezy. When you learn to put God on a higher plane than life's challenges, you are keeping the right perspective. Sure, we will all encounter challenges, struggles, and a host of other distractions that Satan loves to throw at us, but we remember that there is no problem too difficult for God. When you learn to make God bigger than your problems, you will live a much more peaceful life. Now this doesn't happen overnight. You must keep that never give up, never give in attitude and persevere. The same way you didn't learn to walk overnight once your mother gave birth to you; this is a process as well. You will see it gets easier once you have had experiences with God. Keep the right perspective and believe that God only wants the best for you.

For those of you that are into watching the stars and the planets, you most likely own a telescope. A telescope is defined this way, "a usually tubular optical instrument for viewing distant objects by means of the refraction of light rays through a lens or the reflection of light rays by a concave mirror." - https://ww w.merriam-webster.com/dictionary/telescope.

When you look through a telescope, you look through the small glass which is called the eyepiece. I heard a story once about a little boy and a telescope that went like this. There was this boy who was constantly bullied in school by this other boy who was much bigger than him. The little boy was constantly picked on and badgered by this bigger boy. One night the little boy's father came into his room and saw him looking out of his telescope and said to him, "son you are looking out of the telescope in the wrong way. You must look through the eyepiece, not the big wide lens. The little boy just looked at his father. The father came to him and looked at the telescope and saw that he was looking at the bully across the street. The father said, son I don't understand. The little boy replied I am looking through the telescope this way because when I look through the big lens, I see the bully as small and so then he is not so intimidating to me.

When you change your perspective in life and realize that you and God together are a majority and no matter how much rain falls on a just person they will always rise above and never sink like they are in quicksand which is what happens to a just person you will live a life of peace and victory. Check your perspective daily.

Complaining

Complaining is the exact opposite of gratitude. When you don't have a thankful heart, how can you expect God to prosper you? If every time you open your mouth, all you do is gripe, complain, and speak negativity, you will never live a fruitful life. Good fruit produces a harvest, while rotten fruit brings you to a wasteland.

In an article written by TalentSmartEQ by Dr. Travis Bradberry who is the award-winning coauthor of Emotional Intelligence 2.0 and the cofounder of TalentSmartEQ® the world's leading provider of emotional intelligence tests and training he states, "Repeated complaining rewires your brain to make future complaining more likely. Over time, you find it's easier to be negative than to be positive, regardless of what's happening around you. Complaining becomes your default behavior, which changes how people perceive you. And here's the kicker: complaining damages other areas of your brain as well. Research from Stanford University has shown that complaining shrinks the hippocampus—an area of the brain that's critical to problem solving and intelligent thought. Damage to the hippocampus is scary, especially when you consider that it's one of the primary brain areas destroyed by Alzheimer's. While it's not an exaggeration to say that complaining leads to brain damage, it doesn't stop there. When you complain, your body releases the stress hormone cortisol. Cortisol shifts you into fight-or-flight mode, directing oxygen, blood, and energy away from everything but the systems that are essential to immediate survival. One effect of cortisol, for example, is to raise your blood pressure and blood sugar so that you'll be prepared to either escape or defend yourself. All the extra cortisol released by frequent complaining impairs your immune system and makes you more susceptible to high cholesterol, diabetes, heart disease, and obesity. It even makes the brain more vulnerable to strokes."

The Bible depicts an obvious message of how complaining deprives you of success. The children of Israel complained, murmured about various things, including the manna God provided for them. They should have entered the promise land within 11 days. Instead, it took forty years and ultimately of the two million people, only two from the older generation made it into the promise land, which was Caleb and Joshua.

We also see another example in the Bible of someone who never complained, no matter what curve balls were thrown in his direction. This person was Joseph. His brothers threw him into a pit, sold him to a caravan of Pharoah's men, threw him in prison because he was falsely accused of trying to seduce Pharaoh's wife. The cupbearer when he was released from jail forgot him. The cupbearer was supposed to speak to Pharoah about Joseph and try to get him released from jail. With all this rain that fell on this just man Joseph he never complained. What was the outcome? In God's appointed time, Joseph was finally released from jail and put second in command behind Pharoah in Egypt.

Not complaining blesses the life of a just man, so why not try it out? The next time you are tempted to complain, reverse it with gratitude and thankfulness.

"Be thankful for what you have; you'll end up having more. If you concentrate on what you don't have, you will never, ever have enough."

—Oprah Winfrey

"Reflect upon your present blessings—of which every man has many—not on your past misfortunes, of which all men have some."

—Charles Dickens

"When you are grateful, fear disappears, and abundance appears."

—Anthony Robbins

"The soul that gives thanks can find comfort in everything; the soul that complains can find comfort in nothing."

—Hannah Whitall Smith

Abase and Abounding

What does it mean to be abase? According to the dictionary, it means to lower in rank, office, prestige, or esteem. http://www.merriam-webster.com.

What does it mean to be abounding? According to the dictionary, it means existing in or providing a great or plentiful quantity or supply. http://www.merriam-webster.com.

We all in life at one time or another will have highs and lows. Truthfully, we should expect it because it will befall all of us. This is what is meant when we hear the rain falls on the just and the unjust. Don't think just because you consider yourself to be a just person that makes you exempt from the rain and the challenges of life. The only perfect man to walk this earth was Jesus, and he had his share of highs and lows. Some examples of the high points in Jesus' life were when he changed the water to wine and when he raised Lazarus from the dead. These were the abounding times in his life. The low points or abase times were when he was being tempted by Satan in the wilderness for forty days and when he had to suffer crucifixion and death on the cross.

In all the abase times in Jesus' life, he never sinned. The Bible says, "For we have not an high priest which cannot be touched with the feeling of our infirmities; but was in all points tempted like as we are, yet without sin."–Hebrews 4:15. Also, the Bible states "For he hath made him to be sin for us, who knew no sin; that we might be made the righteousness of God in him."–2 Corinthians 5:21. When everything is going smoothly in our lives, and we don't have a care in the world, those are the times we should be aware and on guard and keep doing the godly things. The Bible says, "Be sober, be vigilant; because your adversary the devil, as a roaring lion, walketh about, seeking whom he may devour." -1 Peter 5:8. When things are great, we become complacent and stop doing the right and proper things we should be doing. We stop praying unceasingly and don't go to church regularly because we say to ourselves, we are too busy. This is where we begin to sin because we are moving away from the intimate relationship we are to have with Jesus.

When we reach the low times in our lives and are abase, this is when we know Jesus the most. We pray to God daily, sometimes even hourly. We dust off our Bible and read every day unceasingly. We prepare our clothes for church days before because we are desperate to have the pastor pray all our troubles away. What happens when we do these things, and nothing has changed? These are the times that we need to remember that nothing lasts forever, including trouble. This is when we must remember the words of Paul, "I know both how to be abased, and I know how to abound: everywhere and in all things, I am instructed both to be full and to be hungry, both to abound and to suffer need."–Philippians 4:12 We all pray and speak. "I want to be just like Jesus" however, when God starts to test us and put us on the potter's wheel to refine us, we all start screaming and crying "no stop, take me off." God hears us but continues his work until he has removed what was impure and refined us. "Behold, I have refined thee, but not with silver; I have chosen thee in the furnace of affliction."–Isaiah 48:10.

Everyone would love to have short testing, molding, and refining times, but that is not how God works. The Bible states, "To everything there is a season, and a time to every purpose under the heaven: A time to be born, and a time to die; a time to plant, and a time to pluck up that which is planted; a time to kill, and a time to heal; a time to break down, and a time to build up; a time to weep, and a time to laugh; a time to mourn, and a time to dance; a time to cast away stones, and a time to gather stones together; a time to embrace, and a time to refrain from embracing; A time to get, and a time to lose; a time to keep, and a time to cast away; a time to rend, and a time to sew; a time to keep silence, and a time to speak; a time to love, and a time to hate; a time of war, and a time of peace."–Ecclesiastes 3:1-8.

The verse that I really want you all to see is this one "A time to plant, and a time to pluck up that which is planted." I am not a farmer; I am a city girl, but even I know the principals of planting and harvest. You must plant the seeds and then wait for a harvest. In between, there is watering and pruning. This takes me back to what I said earlier when we are in our low times and are abase this is when we become complacent. The watering is the reading of the word and praying unceasingly. The pruning is what God is doing to us. He is cutting back things in us that are unfruitful and shaping us for a more fruitful growth. These are the times when we feel pain, when we cry, when we don't see where the light at the end of the tunnel is. We have all been there and if you are a person who is a type A personality like me you want the uncomfortableness to go away quickly.

If Jesus, when he was here on earth over 2000 years ago, had to endure the rain and he was the only perfectly just man that ever lived, what makes you think you are exempt? The rain falls on the just and the unjust.

No Blueprint

Blueprint: a photographic print in white on a bright blue ground or blue on a white ground used especially for copying maps, mechanical drawings, and architects' plans. - https://www.merriam-webster.com/dictionary/blueprint

Two of the well-known professions architects and engineers use blueprints. An engineer is a person who designs and builds things for the benefit of society. Engineers use math and science to design and build structures, equipment, and processes. An architect is a person who develops creative designs for buildings or structures. So, the jobs of an engineer and architect, although similar, vary in some details.

Most of us, however, never really encounter blueprints. The main reason we would ever be interested in them is if we purchased a home. Buyers usually ask for a copy of the land survey and blueprints. Buyers want as much information as they can get their hands on. If the seller has this information available, they will hand it over with the keys for the property at the closing. However, don't expect that where your life is concerned. God does not give us a blueprint for our lives. If he did, then we wouldn't need him. We wouldn't have to have faith. God wants us to lean on him and trust him with the life he gave us.

Here are some Bible verses you can turn to when you get agitated because you don't have a blueprint for your life. The blueprint that God wants you to always go to is called FAITH!

"Have not I commanded thee? Be strong and of a good courage; be not afraid, neither be thou dismayed: for the Lord thy God is with thee whithersoever thou goest." –Joshua 1:9.

"And they that know thy name will put their trust in thee: for thou, Lord, hast not forsaken them that seek thee." –Psalm 9:10.

"Trust in the Lord with all thine heart; and lean not unto thine own understanding. In all thy ways acknowledge him, and he shall direct thy paths." –Proverbs 3:5-6.

"And Jesus answering saith unto them, Have faith in God. For verily I say unto you, that whosoever shall say unto this mountain, be thou removed, and be thou cast into the sea; and shall not doubt in his heart but shall believe that those things which he saith shall come to pass; he shall have whatsoever he saith. Therefore, I say unto you, what things soever ye desire, when ye pray, believe that ye receive them, and ye shall have them." –Mark 11:22-24.

"And Jesus said unto them, Because of your unbelief: for verily I say unto you, If ye have faith as a grain of mustard seed, ye shall say unto this mountain, Remove hence to yonder place, and it shall remove, and nothing shall be impossible unto you." –Matthew 17:20.

"Jesus answered and said unto them, Verily I say unto you, If ye have faith, and doubt not, ye shall not only do this which is done to the fig tree but also if ye shall say unto this mountain, Be thou removed, and be thou cast into the sea; it shall be done." –Matthew 21:21.

"For we walk by faith, not by sight." –2 Corinthians 5:7.

I live in Florida which has several playgrounds like Disney, Universal, Lego Land, SeaWorld, and more. All of them have roller coasters. If you are a fan of roller coasters, you don't ask for the schematics and blueprints before you get on the ride. You just jump on, scream, holler, and enjoy yourself. Life is short, and we are to enjoy this life God gave us. "There is nothing better for a man than that he should eat and drink, and that he should make his soul enjoy good in his labour. This also I saw that it was from the hand of God." -Ecclesiastes 2:24.

Hope

"Now the God of hope fill you with all joy and peace in believing, that ye may abound in hope, through the power of the Holy Ghost." -Romans 15:13.

Let's just take a moment to pick apart some keywords and phrases from the above Bible verse.

God of Hope–If God has hope, who are we not to? God had hope when he created the world and created people, expecting them to take care of it and not sin. When that plan was destroyed because of the sin of Adam and Eve, God had hope again when he had Noah build the arc and commanded him to multiply and reproduce after the floods.

Joy and Peace–God can fill your life with joy and peace no matter how many challenges you are facing. His word clearly states this, "And the peace of God, which passeth all understanding, shall keep your hearts and minds through Christ Jesus." -Philippians 4:7. What does this mean? In essence, it means no more anxiety, depression, worry, sleepless nights, etc.

Believing–I have said this earlier. God expects us to be believers, not achievers. We have a part and God has a part.

Some of the greatest minds knew how important it is to keep believing always, and they spoke on the subject.

"We are born believing. A man bears beliefs as a tree bears apples." - Ralph Waldo Emerson

"Believe and act as if it were impossible to fail." - Charles F. Kettering

"If you believe you can, you probably can. If you believe you won't, you most assuredly won't. Belief is the ignition switch that gets you off the launching pad." - Denis Waitley

"If you believe in what you are doing, then let nothing hold you up in your work. Much of the best work of the world has been done against seeming impossibilities. The thing is to get the work done." - Dale Carnegie

"You can do it if you believe you can." - Napoleon Hill

"Whatever you believe with feeling becomes your reality". - Brian Tracy

Abound—God desires for you to have an abounding life. He says so in his word, "Therefore, my beloved brethren, be ye stedfast, unmoveable, always abounding in the work of the Lord, forasmuch as ye know that your labour is not in vain in the Lord." -1 Corinthians 15:58.

Once we have no hope, we might as well be dead! Hope allows us to dream about what could happen or what could be true. "Hope is the word which GOD has written on the brow of everyman." - Victor Hugo. Victor Marie Hugo was a French poet, novelist, and dramatist of the Romantic Movement. He is considered one of the greatest and best-known French writers. www.wickipedia.com

On holidays such as Memorial Day, Fourth of July, Labor Day, countless people always say this very phrase: "I hope the weather is going to be good because I intend to barbeque." Hope is built in us but, it is up to us whether we choose to ignite the flame. "Without GOD there is for mankind no purpose, no goal, no hope, only a wavering future, an eternal dread of everyday darkness." - Jean Paul (Jean Paul born Johann Paul Friedrich Richter, was a German Romantic writer, best known for his humorous novels and stories). - www.wickipedia.com.

"A child's world is fresh and new and beautiful, full of wonder and excitement. It is our misfortune that for most of us that clear-eyed vision, that true instinct for what is beautiful and awe-inspiring, is dimmed and even lost before we reach adulthood"" Rachel Carson (Rachel Louise Carson was an American marine biologist and conservationist whose book Silent Spring and other writings are credited with advancing the global environmental movement). - www.wickipe dia.com.

We all know the story of Cinderella, a girl, a shoe, and a prince. Cinderella lived an unhappy life as a young girl. Her mother was dead, and her father had married a widow with two daughters. Her stepmother didn't like her one bit and so she made her life miserable. They forced Cinderella to live in poverty while those around her enjoyed the good life, especially her stepsisters. The story of Cinderella teaches us to enjoy simple pleasures, about endurance, and about maintaining an optimistic attitude and holding onto hope. As adults, we need to become more childlike and visualize a tomorrow with endless possibilities. Stir up your hope and watch God catapult your life at warp speed.

Chapter 8

Each Time You Conquer A Step There Will Always Be Another Challenge Waiting

In this journey of life, we should realize that God wants us all to grow, stretch, and mature. Just like newborn babies, we are not to be drinking baby formula all our lives. At some point, we are expected to be eating solid foods. This is the same way believers in God are expected to be. When we are new believers in Christ, we are learning as we go and making mistakes as we go. However, when you have been a believer in God for many years, you should be more mature because of the experiences you have had with God. This is a step-by-step process and there will be challenges along the way.

People who are dancers by profession know what I mean. However, if you enjoy dancing as a hobby, you can also relate. Ballroom dancers are tremendous. Two of the greatest ever were Fred Astaire and Ginger Rogers. They were a fantastic pair and performed ballroom dancing together as partners in ten movies.

For those of you that enjoy ballroom dancing as a hobby or just enjoy watching Dancing with The Stars, there are different dances split mainly into two categories

Smooth and Rhythm. The easiest smooth dance to do is the Waltz. However, once you have mastered that, then there is the next challenge of learning a Viennese Waltz. On the other hand, the easiest rhythm dance to learn is the Rumba, but once that is perfected, then the challenge is to learn the Samba.

This is the journey of life. Once you have mastered something, there will always be another challenge waiting for you. Don't panic, slump your shoulders, and start sinking into the abyss. Remember, you can do all things through Christ, which strengthens you. - Philippians 4:13.

Dream Big

Dream - a visionary; a strongly desired goal or purpose. Something that fully satisfies a wish. - https://www.merriam-webster.com/dictionary/dream

When we are young kids in school, sometimes even as early as when we are in kindergarten, the teacher asks us "what do we want to be when we grow up?" The regular answers range from a doctor, lawyer, teacher, ballerina, police officer, and firefighter. After mom and dad come into our room to kiss us goodnight, we lay awake in bed staring up at the ceiling dreaming about what we said we wanted to become when we grow up.

As we grow older and become adults, the way for some of us becomes a winding road and, sometimes, life gets in the way. The passion for our dreams lifts, up, and away, just like the space shuttle when it leaves Kennedy Space Center. Some of us, unfortunately, take those dreams with us to our graves. Others realize if you are still alive, God has a purpose and a dream for you to fulfill and it doesn't matter how old you are. Start today!

Every four years we are fortunate to watch other's dreams come to life with the Olympics. The 2018 Winter Olympics have come and gone, and it was exciting to see the smiles on people's faces and the stories behind their lives and what they had to overcome to be in the Olympics. The one theme that resonates with all the participants is how grateful they were to be at the Olympics, performing and living their dreams.

One of the people involved was snowboarder Shaun White. When Shaun was born, he was born with a heart defect and had to endure several surgeries. This is something he discussed when he was a guest on the Jimmy Kimmel show when Jimmy spoke about the same heart defect his baby was born with. Shaun spoke openly about how his parents knew that any strenuous activity could cause a problem, but they were never overly protective. Shaun's love for skateboarding and snowboarding grew, and he took part in several Olympics and in 2018 won his third gold medal and became the first snowboarder to win three gold medals at the Olympics.

The same way that God placed a big dream in Joseph's life where he became second in command to Pharoah in Egypt, he has placed a dream inside you. Dream big, visualize it, move towards it and work hard. It will happen even though you may face challenges, or it looks like it will never happen, or you are soaked with rain remember what the Bible says, "Now thanks be unto God, which always causeth us to triumph in Christ, and maketh manifest the savour of his knowledge by us in every place." -2 Corinthians 2:14.

Believe

The definition of the word BELIEVE states - to have a firm conviction as to the goodness, efficacy, or ability of something. A psychological state in which an individual holds a proposition or premise to be true. Religious belief, a belief regarding the supernatural, sacred, or divine. https://www.merriam-webster.co m/dictionary/believe

"Verily, verily, I say unto you, He that believeth on me hath everlasting life." -John 6:47

"That if thou shalt confess with thy mouth the Lord Jesus, and shalt believe in thine heart that God hath raised him from the dead, thou shalt be saved." -Romans 10:9

"And all things, whatsoever ye shall ask in prayer, believing, ye shall receive." -Matthew 21:22

"For God so loved the world, that he gave his only begotten Son, that whoso-ever believeth in him should not perish, but have everlasting life." -John 3:16

"Now the God of hope fill you with all joy and peace in believing, that ye may abound in hope, through the power of the Holy Ghost." -Romans 15:13

"For with the heart man believeth unto righteousness, and with the mouth confession is made unto salvation." -Romans 10:10

"But without faith it is impossible to please him: for he that cometh to God must believe that he is and that he is a rewarder of them that diligently seek him." -Hebrews 11:6

The Bible says, "And we know that all things work together for good to them that love God, to them who are the called according to his purpose." –Romans 8:28. Abraham believed this that is why he was not shaken or filled with anxiety when the angel of the Lord told him to take his son Isaac up into the mountain and kill him. Isaac is the son Abraham and Sarah waited 25 years to have. Since Abraham was prepared with knife in hand to kill the one thing he desperately wanted and waited a quarter of a century to have God told him to stop and do not harm Isaac and then a ram appeared in the bushes for Abraham to kill instead.

Since Abraham could believe so solidly in God and his word, we should do the same. The Lord blessed him because he believed. God can turn things around in a moment's notice to our benefit. We just must believe. As you can see, the Bible has an enormous amount to say about believing.

Let's look at a breakdown of the word believe.

B = Begin - to give attention to something. We should all start our day with prayer, thanksgiving, and gratitude because we know not when our time is up. "For man also knoweth not his time: as the fishes that are taken in an evil net, and as the birds that are caught in the snare; so are the sons of men snared in an evil time, when it falleth suddenly upon them." -Ecclesiastes 9:12

E = Emulate - to try to be like (someone or something you admire).

If we say we want to be like Christ so we can get to heaven, then we need to copy his ways. "He that saith he abideth in him ought himself also so to walk, even as he walked." -1 John 2:6

L = Love - a feeling of strong or constant affection for a person. The object of attachment, devotion, or admiration. GOD commands us to love one another. "A new commandment I give unto you, that ye love one another; as I have loved you, that ye also love one another. - John 13:34. And now abideth faith, hope, charity, these three; but the greatest of these is charity." -1 Corinthians 13:13

I = Invest - to involve or engage, especially emotionally. We are to invest time in our walk with GOD. "But his delight is in the law of the Lord, and in his law doth he meditate day and night." -Psalm 1:2. "See then that ye walk circumspectly, not as fools, but as wise, redeeming the time, because the days are evil." -Ephesians 5:15-16

E = Endure - to regard with acceptance or tolerance. To undergo especially without giving in. Unfortunately, now too often we hear of someone committing suicide. If we are to emulate Christ, then we are to endure. "Looking unto Jesus the author and finisher of our faith, who for the joy that was set before him endured the cross, despising the shame, and is set down at the right hand of the throne of God." -Hebrews 12:2

V = Vision - something that you imagine. A picture that you see in your mind. If you want to keep your belief in something, you should have a vision board. Put up pictures of the things you want to achieve and keep it close so you will always keep striving and reaching. "Where there is no vision, the people perish: but he that keepeth the law, happy is he." -Proverbs 29:18.

E -= Enjoy - to take pleasure in something. To have or experience (something good or helpful). It is important for you to enjoy your life and to do that; you need a proper balance. That is what God wants for you. "The thief comes only in order to steal and kill and destroy. I came that they may have and enjoy life, and have it in abundance to the full, till it overflows." -John 10:10

When you feel like you can't go on and the rains are beating and battering you and you feel you don't deserve it because you are a believer and a just person remember you are stronger than you think and God has something much bigger, better, and brighter ahead so go for it - BELIEVE - BELIEVE - BELIEVE.

Favor

Every day of our lives, we all receive the favor of God in one way or another. If God provides you with the breath of life, that is your first favor of the day. A lot of us think God owes us something. Wrong! God doesn't owe us anything. However, he wants to rain down favor on our lives. Favor can come in many forms and fashions. Sometimes when we are prideful, we just believe that favor must be some huge outlandish thing, but not always. A lot of times, the smaller favors mean more than the bigger ones. God knows the right time to bless you with small favor as well as when to bless you with large portions of favor. Sometimes we think we are ready for the big stuff and God knows if he bestows it on us, we will crumble under the weight of it because we are just not ready yet.

Has any of these situations ever happened to you?

a) - You pay a bill, but then you forgot about it until you see it has posted to your bank account before your payroll. Miraculously, you don't get a bank fee charge for overdraft or insufficient funds.

b) - You're in a hurry and you're speeding. The police pull you over. You know the drill license and registration. You forgot your license at home. The police officer asks for your name, address, and date of birth. Now you sit and wait for an eternity as if you weren't in a rush in the beginning. Miraculously, when the officer returns to your car, he says your info checks out; you don't have any warrants or outstanding tickets, so I'm going to let you go with a warning.

c) - You rush out of the house to pick up your child from school, but you forgot you left a pot on the stove boiling. You immediately make a U-turn and head back to your home. Miraculously, the pot has boiled out, and the contents of the pot have started to burn, but no smoke or fire has started.

THESE ARE ALL EXAMPLES OF THE FAVOR OF GOD!

How do you attract the favor of God? Well, two things stand out quickly. You need to have a humble heart and show repentance for any sin you have committed.

This is what King David did in the Bible and that is why he received favor from God when King Saul did not. Both men had sinned drastically, but Saul had prideful ways and didn't give God the glory he deserves. David, however, did, and they recorded this in the Bible where he says, "And I will delight myself in thy commandments, which I have loved. My hands also will I lift up unto thy commandments, which I have loved; and I will meditate in thy statutes." -Psalms 119:47-48

"The Miracle on the Hudson" is another example of the favor of God. On January 15, 2009, an Airbus A320 was in flight and was struck by a flock of birds that caused severe damage to both plane's engines, which caused them to stop working. The men in charge were first office Jeffrey Bruce Skiles, who immediately configured an engine restart while the captain Sully Sullenberger glided the plane to a safe landing spot on the Hudson and all 155 passengers survived and were rescued by nearby boats.

If this is not the favor of God, I DON'T KNOW WHAT IS! Do we know if every passenger on the plane was a believer in God? No, we don't. However, if there were only a select few that believed in God, then we have another example of how the rain falls on the just and the unjust. The rains came, but they all survived.

Chapter 9

The Journey

Every one of us in life is on a journey. The problem lies because we are mainly concerned about getting to the destination instead of enjoying the journey. God is concerned about our journey, as well as our destination.

The journey comprises several things. You will encounter some straight paths, but they will be few and far between. You, however, will encounter many steep hills, mountains, winding roads, and cliffhangers. Writers, especially fiction writers, will know what I mean when I say cliff hanger. The definition of a cliff hanger is an adventure serial or melodrama, especially one presented in installments, each ending in suspense. https://www.merriam-webster.com/dictionary/cliff-hanger.

The journey of our lives builds our character. We build our strength. It shows us we are stronger than we think. We can see our weaknesses. It shows how strong your faith is. It divulges where your heart lies. The journey shows whether you are a prideful person or a person of humility who knows they can do nothing by themselves. It is all because of God. Do you think I believe I can write this book without the help of God? I could not complete one sentence if I was not relying on God and praying for his anointing to execute this.

If we allow it, the journey will mature us. The journey is a concept as old as time. The children of Israel went on a journey when they left Pharoah. It was supposed to be an eleven-day trip, but because all they did was grumble and complain, it took forty years instead. All our journeys are different with a different time span. There are some of us that unfortunately, when we are taken from our mother's womb, we are dead. Then there are some of us that live a few good years and then pass away. At the time of the writing of this book, producer extraordinaire Norman Lear who produced so many fabulous shows like "All in the Family", "The Jeffersons", "One Day At A Time" etc. just celebrated his 100th birthday. Some journeys are longer than others, but it is very important that we learn to enjoy the journey with all it offers.

Will the journey have rain? Of course, it will. It will encounter all four seasons of life, but they all have a lesson to be learned. The more battles you encounter on the journey, means that God has a huge future for you. Don't complain about the journey and sit on the sidelines because you believe it is too tough. Do what the Bible says, "Put on the whole armour of God, that ye may be able to stand against the wiles of the devil. For we wrestle not against flesh and blood, but against principalities, against powers, against the rulers of the darkness of this world, against spiritual wickedness in high places. Wherefore take unto you the whole armour of God, that ye may be able to withstand in the evil day, and having done all, to stand." -Ephesians 6:11-13.

God Is In The Miracle Working Business

When Jesus was here on earth, he did a ton of miracles from changing water into wine to raising Lazarus from the dead. Just because Jesus left over 2,000 years ago, don't think that miracles no longer happen. If you are at a stage in your life where you need a miracle, just ask God for it. Remember, the Bible says, "Ye lust, and have not: ye kill, and desire to have, and cannot obtain: ye fight and war, yet ye have not, because ye ask not. Ye ask, and receive not, because ye ask amiss, that ye may consume it upon your lusts." - James 4:2.

A read a story awhile back in 2016 from the town of Galt in Sacramento County entitled 'Freeway Miracle?' which was an astounding story of a German Shepard dog who fell off the back of her owner's truck on highway 90 that survived 5 weeks with 2 broken bones. How the dog survived is anybody's guess. Surviving without food or water for 5 weeks is more than likely physically impossible. Yet the dog, nicknamed 'Freeway Frida', did just that. The dog was subsequently rescued and was taken to the Bradshaw Veterinary Clinic and underwent surgery. She only weighed 44 pounds when she was found on the highway. The Galt police department tried tirelessly to locate her family, but no one came forward. Frida was treated for the injuries and was adopted by Officer Coelho of the Galt police department after three months. Many people believe it is a bona fide miracle. It very well may be.

A story on the CNN website by Manisha Ganguly back in 2018 presented the story of newborn Vanellope Hope Wilkins who was born with her heart outside her body in Leicester, UK. Against all odds, the baby survived after three surgeries to place the heart inside her chest. According to the article, many such cases result in termination of pregnancy or stillbirth. The odds of survival come in at less than 10%. If a case can be made for the existence of miracles in the modern day, this would be a perfect example.

Colton Dixon, who is an American Christian rock, singer-songwriter and musician who was on season 11 of American Idol, also has a personal story of miracles in his life. Colton says that his wife carried twin girls for 38 weeks back in 2020 with no problems. He said his wife Annie never got sick once during the pregnancy. However, things changed drastically when it was time for Annie to give birth. Something went wrong during a C-section and one of the twin girls, Dior was born without a pulse. According to Colton, it was a moment in his life that required "faith over fear." There was a lot of chaos in the delivery room and Colton and Annie prayed to God to step in and spare their daughter's life. They prayed for God's plan for her life to come true and not let the enemy's plan come true, which is to steal, kill, and destroy. Dior is now a healthy baby two years later, just like her sister.

God is still in the miracle working business and all you must do is have faith, trust, and believe. Remember, God built you tough, so no matter what challenges, obstacles, or rain comes into your life, you are stronger than you think and will arise victoriously.

New Level New Devil

Are you trusting God and praying big, bold, huge payers? I mean the type of prayers that only God can answer. If you are praying for something that you feel you can handle and get on your own, then they are small prayers. I mean prayers that are jaw dropping. As you are looking to expand your horizons and level up, you will encounter many tests and challenges. This is what we call New Level New Devil.

We all have a long laundry list, especially if we pray bold prayers to God of the things we want, the things we want to accomplish, and the legacy we want to leave in life. The Bible says, "Ask, and it shall be given you; seek, and ye shall find; knock, and it shall be opened unto you.'–Matthew 7:7.

The same way God has a plan for your life, so does the devil. His agenda is to thwart all the grand plans God has for your future. If you get frustrated, annoyed, and unhappy with the challenges, then Satan wins. Picture an Iron Man competition where several men are pulling on a rope trying to get the advantage and pull down the opposite competitors. This is what it is with God and Satan. God and his angels are pulling for you to follow God's path which will bring you to victory while Satan and his army and trying to destroy you with fear, worry, anxiety, anger, bitterness, unforgiveness, and a host of other distractions to get your eyes off God.

When you make a choice to follow God, get ready. If you think Satan is just going to lie down and allow you to pass, you are sorely mistaken. Here is a good gauge for your life: If you aren't having any issues, struggles, challenges, then unfortunately you are not a concern to Satan. Once you are a concern, he will throw every curve ball your way and try to not only knock you down but also knock you out. Think about two people bowling one hits a gutter ball and the other a strike where all the pins fall. That is what Satan is trying to do to you. If, on the other hand, you are following God, then "fasten your seatbelts." This was a signature line from the Hall of Fame broadcaster Bob Murphy for the NY Mets baseball team that he would say during tight games.

God is waiting to be gracious and grant you the things you are asking for, but they first must line up with the job he placed you on this earth to accomplish and secondly, you must be ready and prepared to step into that position. When God knows you are not ready, not mature enough to handle what you are asking for, he will not give it to you. When God had Moses take command and take the children of Israel from Pharaoh and deliver them from slavery and bondage, he did not take them on the easy, quick course. The travel time into the promise land should have only been an eleven-day trip, but because God knew this group of over two million people were not ready, he took them the long route which wound up being a forty-year journey. Another reason the journey took so long is because of all the complaining the congregation kept doing. Gratitude will bless your life while complaining will destroy it. Instead of being grateful that they were finally free after all the years of bondage, all they did was complain. They complained about the same food manna every day, no water to drink, etc. to Moses all the time. God has a sense of humor and when he sends tests your way and you keep failing, he will not give you the desires of your heart. You must trust him, become mature and pass the tests and challenges.

For those of you that are parents, you will understand this example. You purchase a new car, and your child is in love with it. The color, the new car smell, the wheels, the interior, etc. They ask you if they can drive the car. Knowing all the pitfalls and negative things that could happen since they are only sixteen years old, you say no. This is the same process with God. He knows everything and he will not let you elevate to the next level if you are not ready for it because of the challenges and devils you will encounter. New devils come in all shapes and sizes. One example could be that you become a manager for a group of 50 people, and you feel very prideful because you got the promotion over other people, so you throw your weight around. No. this is the incorrect behavior so since God knows what you will do before even you do; he will not elevate you to the next level. You could pray to become a highly successful author which will have you doing many speaking engagements and book signings, but you have an issue with handling criticism badly. Not everyone will think you're great and so you will come across critics, and you must be mature enough to handle that. You can't go tit for tat with every person who doesn't like you. Promotion is a beautiful thing but remember New Level New Devil.

The Goodness Of God

Goodness is the state or quality of being good, moral excellence; virtue, kindly feeling; kindness; generosity, excellence of quality, the best part of anything; essence; strength. - http://www.dictionary.com

The goodness of God is not only an attribute of God but a foundational truth every Christian should embrace and one that is found in most Christian books. "No person can be his own savior...An individual must come before God in penitence, confess his sin and obtain pardon from a merciful God who repudiates sin but shows covenant love to the sinner." - R. K. Harrison (was an Old Testament Scholar). Instead of a river, God often gives us a brook, which may be running today and dried up tomorrow. Why? To teach us not to rest in our blessings, but in the blesser Himself. - Arthur Pink (was an English Bible teacher who sparked a renewed interest in the exposition of Calvinism. This is a major branch of Protestantism that follows the theological tradition and forms of Christian practice of John Calvin and other reformation - era theologians. Pink became one of the most influential evangelical authors in the second half of the twentieth century). https://en.wikipedia.org/wiki/Arthur_Pink

There isn't a single person reading this now who hasn't experienced outrageous, lavish, unexpected, undeserved kindness. Also, we experience these serendipities every single day. They are poured out over us constantly. I know I have. At one time or another, most of us have been driving and look in our rearview mirror and see those blue flashing lights. Our hearts palpitate, and we know what we're in for. That happened to me about 7 years ago. I was running late and needed to make time, and the police officer pulled me over. You know the routine: license and registration. I had just been to the bank the previous day and needed to present my license for withdrawal and forgot to put it back in my wallet. That made the stop with the officer even longer because now I had to provide my DOB and have him check for tickets, warrants, etc. Eventually he returned to my car and gave me a monologue about all the tickets he could have given me doing 65 in a 45 zone, no license, etc. instead he gave me a warning and let me go. That is an example of the goodness of God.

Now, you may not have a story like mine, but every day we all receive goodness from God. You may have noticed a sale at your local supermarket, pharmacy, clothing or shoe store and then life got in the way, and you didn't make it there on the dates. You stop by anyway and notice that the sale signs are still listed and the store personnel states they will give you the items at the sales price anyway because it was their error that the signs weren't removed. That is an example of the goodness of God. Your friend has a big birthday party the night before you have a doctor's appt and you forgot about the appointment and stay out late eating past the bewitching hour. Once you return home, you check your date planner on the refrigerator and see the scheduled appointment. You are going for your second A1C testing and have been advised if the numbers don't add up, you will need to go on medication. Now you can't sleep, and you're worried about what the test results will be. You go to the doctor's and do your testing and now you wait for the results. After a few days, you are told everything looks fine. WOW! Relief sweeps over you because you know that all your proper eating and managing yourself did not go to waste in one night. That is an example of the goodness of God.

The Goodness of God covers us all, not just believers and the just. Remember, God is no respecter of persons but we as believers and just people have a special covering when the rain comes in our lives as struggles, challenges, tests, that just like Rain-X the windshield glass water repellent that dramatically improves visibility when you are driving in wet weather our repellant is God. He makes sure the plan of Satan never destroys us.

Chapter 10

You Are God's Masterpiece

People that are painters and sculptors are very gifted people. Some of the greatest paintings and sculptors are hanging in some of the most famous museums in the world. The Louvre in Paris, France has The Mona Lisa, Venus de Milo, & Bathsheba at Her Bath. The last one was the woman King David married and had her husband Uriah the Hittite killed, which angered God and once Bathsheba became pregnant with King David's child, God advised him that the child would not live because of the evil he did. The Prado Museum in Madrid Spain houses portraits of Adam & Eve, Christ Crucified, & The Seven Deadly Sins.

One of the greatest sculptors ever know was Michelangelo. It is stated that Michelangelo's greatest masterpiece is the statue of David, which is located at Accademia Gallery of Florence (Galleria dell'Accademia di Firenze) in Florence Italy. Trust me, it is breathtaking when you walk up and see it face to face. It has been stated that "Sculpture is considered the finest art form because it mimics divine creation. The sculptural image is found within the block of stone much as the human soul is found within the physical body." - https://www.pbs.org/wg bh/cultureshock/flashpoints/visualarts/david_at.html

In the New Living Translation Bible, it says, "For we are God's masterpiece. He has created us anew in Christ Jesus, so we can do the good things he planned for us long ago." —Ephesians 2:10. Since the Bible is the true word, and it says you are God's masterpiece, you must see yourself that way. This applies even when you are going through trials, struggles, and challenges of all sorts. God has a glorious life planned for you, but to step into it, you must believe. God is constantly molding and shaping all of us to be what he wants us to be and step into the splendid plans he has for us all.

Don't allow the rain that comes your way to stop you from becoming all you were created to be. Getting mad and angry at God only delays what he has for you. Remember what I said earlier: God has a plan for your life and so does Satan, and they are both working very hard. When you allow Satan to distract you and you turn away from God, he will just stand off to the side until you are ready to recommit to being all he created you to be. God gave us choices when he created the world, and we still have those choices. Don't let the rain coming down on you as a just person anger you and make you prideful because you feel that rain should only come down on unjust people and allow it to distract you from your glorious future. You are God's masterpiece!

Be Yourself

"Be yourself; everyone else is already taken." —— Oscar Wilde

"To be yourself in a world that is constantly trying to make you something else is the greatest accomplishment." —— Ralph Waldo Emerson

"Always be a first-rate version of yourself and not a second-rate version of someone else." —— Judy Garland

God created each one of us in his own image. He gave each one of us specific gifts to be used to accomplish what he wanted us to do with the life he gave us. Each one of us is God's masterpiece. Do you know what a masterpiece is? It is a person's greatest piece of work, as in art. Anything done with masterly skill: a consummate example of skill or excellence of any kind: a piece made by a person aspiring to the rank of master in a guild or other craft organization as a proof of competence. - http://Dictionary.com.

Instead of being ourselves, we are always comparing ourselves to others. We are always saying things like:

I wish I was pretty like her/him.

Look at his/her physique. Why can't I look like that?

I want to sing as she/he does.

Why can't I dance as they do?

Look how long and silky his/her hair is. Why can't mine be like that?

Why can't my teeth be straight and bright white like his/hers is?

How come I don't have the same metabolism he/she does? They can eat anything they want and gain no weight.

I wish I was as talented as he/she is.

I would give anything to be as smart and educated as he/she is.

Why wasn't I born as tall as he/she is?

I know if I had been given a better personality than he/she has, I would be further off in life.

We don't realize how much we hurt God when we want to be a duplicate of someone else. You are an original. If you don't think so, remember that when there is a horrific fire, and the deceased cannot be identified because they have been burned so badly the one sure way of obtaining an identification so they can notify the next of kin is with fingerprints. God made sure that none of us have identical fingerprints, so that should tell you something. Also, the gifts that he has placed in each one of us are not the same. He created you deliberately to be different and so you should be proud of that and not try to be a duplicate of someone else. Remember the story of David when he went to fight Goliath? King Saul gave him all his armor and told him to put them on and wear them, but after he did, David was so uncomfortable and walked awkwardly that he told King Saul this was not for me. I can do this with God. Remember, you and God are a majority!

Find & Utilize Your Happy Place

Are you feeling overwhelmed, stressed out, and just downright exasperated with life? If so, just take a few deep breaths, make a list of at least 10 things you are grateful for, and then find and utilize your happy place. Your happy place is where you travel with your mind and feel good, where you are relaxed and can be positive. It is a place that is safe, secure, and problem-free.

In our brain, we have two types of neurotransmitters called dopamine and serotonin. When we are happy, both are released and bring us joy. Some of the health benefits of feeling happy and joyful are it promotes a healthier lifestyle, boosts your immune system, fights stress and pain, and supports longevity. Think about how you feel when you are cradling your favorite breed of puppy. Close your eyes and imagine that scene. Imagine running your hands on their coat of fur, looking into their puppy eyes, watching them yawn, all priceless images. No doubt these things will make you happy. Now if you are not a dog person, then imagine these happy feelings with whatever type of animal you adore.

Today, there are so many things that can stress us out and keep us wound up like a ball of yarn. However, remember, God did not create us to be this way. Remember, God said. "Beloved, I wish above all things that thou mayest prosper and be in health, even as thy soul prospereth. –3 John 2. When we are prospering, we are happy, joyful, elated, ecstatic, relaxed, and thriving. If God wants these things for us, we should want them for ourselves and aspire to reach these heights.

When we are so frustrated, wound up, anxious, judgmental, we are only hurting ourselves. Health is the most important thing you can have because when it is debilitated, all the money in the world cannot miraculously bring it back. They say that anger weakens the liver, grief weakens the lungs, worry weakens the stomach, stress weakens the heart and brain, and fear fails the kidneys. When we are complaining and criticizing God because we believe we are a just person, so why are we having all this rain fall on us and cause all this turbulence in our lives we are only making matters worse. The quicker we reverse our behavior and start having gratitude that God gives you the grace to endure and praising him the faster things will turn around.

What does your happy place consist of in your mind? Remember, every day we are all fighting the Battlefield of the Mind. Joyce Meyer always says, "where the mind goes, the man follows." So does your happy place consist of lying in a hammock swinging back and forth, attending a world premiere for a movie you starred in, receiving a Pulitzer prize award for your writing accomplishments, vacationing in Hawaii, spending quality time with family, watching a Hallmark movie, driving your convertible car with the top down, getting a full body massage, immersing your toes in the white sand on a beach, skydiving, canoeing, skiing, driving your own yacht, baking gingerbread cookies for the holidays, quilting a bedspread, attending a smooth jazz cruise, playing golf, enjoying a game of darts, visualizing being debt-free etc.

We all have things that make us happy, bring a smile to our face, and relax our body. Find those places and go to them as often as you can because it will keep you balanced, relaxed, and happy where you can stay positive and remember that God wants the best for you all the days of your life. We need very little to make a happy life; it is all within yourself, in your way of thinking. - Marcus Aurelius Antoninus.

The Amusement Arcade

An amusement arcade (often referred to as a video arcade or simply arcade) is a venue where people play arcade games such as video games, pinball machines, electro-mechanical games, redemption games, merchandisers (such as claw cranes), or coin-operated billiards or air hockey tables. In some countries, some types of arcades are also legally permitted to provide gambling machines, such as slot machines or pachinko machines. Games are usually housed in cabinets. The term used for ancestors of these venues in the beginning of the 20th century was penny arcades. Video games were introduced in amusement arcades in the late 1970s and were most popular during the golden age of arcade video games. - https://en.wikipedia.org/wiki/Amusement_arcade.

Amusement Arcades have been beloved for years. These places are where people can have fun, laugh, test their skills and much more. Amusement Arcades have a plethora of choices. My favorite is Skeeball, but there are a variety of things to enjoy. Amusement Arcades were taken to an elevated level when Dave & Busters was founded in Dallas TX in 1982. This establishment not only has a video arcade in all their locations, but they also have a full-service restaurant. Now people can dine and have fun at the same time. People have so many choices of the games to entertain themselves.

Daily we also have so many choices to do the right thing and live a godly life instead of a sinful life. Are we going to have faith or are we going to live in fear? We have the choice to trust God or be a doubting Thomas. "The other disciples therefore said unto him, we have seen the Lord. But he said unto them, Except I shall see in his hands the print of the nails and put my finger into the print of the nails, and thrust my hand into his side, I will not believe."–John 20:25. Will we believe that we have the power, strength, and determination to handle any challenge that comes our way? The Bible says," I can do all things through Christ which strengtheneth me."–Philippians 4:13. Are we willing to live a life based on integrity? Will we choose daily to bless our family, friends, and people with our words and not speak ill of them? Are we willing to be Good Samaritans? As parents, we can be like the father of The Prodigal Son who wasted all his inheritance and came humbly begging his father to take him back as a hired hand? When you go grocery shopping, will you return the grocery cart to the appointed place or just leave it anywhere where it can roll and hit someone's vehicle and cause damage?

It is very important that in this journey of life that you take time for yourself. If you are constantly at the beck and call for someone else, you will eventually burn out and then you are no good to yourself or anyone else. We get a clear picture of this in the Bible with Mary & Martha. Martha was constantly busy with many things, but Mary just sat at Jesus' feet. The more time we sit with God and look to cultivate an intimate relationship with him, the easier we will manage when the rains of life come down on us or dump a deluge on us, we feel we don't deserve because we are a just person.

If you believe that you are a just person, then you should take it as a compliment when the rainstorms of life appear at your door because that means God knows you can handle it. Not only is God by your side for everything, keep this in mind never complain about the rain or the difficulties in life, because a director (GOD) always gives the hardest roles to his best actors!

Laughter

Laughter... it seems like such a simple thing to do; however, it isn't especially if you are an adult. Children find it easy to laugh. They chuckle about everything. It is said children laugh on average 200 times a day. However, on the contrary, adults only laugh 4 times per day. As adults, we have allowed ourselves to get lost in the stress of life. We don't take time to have fun anymore. There are deadlines, time crunches, agendas, etc. Adults have lost the capacity to do as it is stated in the Bible: "A merry heart doeth good like a medicine: but a broken spirit drieth the bones."–Proverbs 17:22.

It has always amazed me at how comedians can get up on stage and start telling jokes and make you laugh so hard and forget all of life's concerns. They have a tremendous gifting to make people laugh and the health benefits that it does for our bodies are truly the wonders of God. Then there are the ventriloquists that work with puppets. One of the most blessed ones is Jeff Dunham and his puppets. It takes so many years and the blessing of God to craft your work so well that you have sold-out audiences all over the world.

Laughter is medicine! The best part of that is that is doesn't cost us anything. When is the last time you filled a prescription for medicine and there was no charge? Maybe the medicine somehow didn't cost but for you to get the prescription, you had to go through the doctor and there was a co-pay you were responsible for.

God laughed. Here are some bible verses regarding that:

"He that sitteth in the heavens shall laugh: the Lord shall have them in derision". –Psalm 2:4

"The Lord shall laugh at him: for he seeth that his day is coming." –Psalm 37:13

"But You, O LORD, laugh at them; You scoff at all the nations." –Psalm 59:8

So, if God laughed knowing its benefits, and we were created in his likeness, then we should also laugh.

Here are some benefits of laughter:

Relaxes the whole body

Increases blood flow

Creates oxygenation of the cells and organs

Defends against illness

Provides greater memory, intelligence, and creativity

Is a pain killer

Boosts the immune system

Triggers the release of endorphins

Lightens anger's heavy load

It may even help you live longer

The Physical Health Benefits of Laughter:

Boosts Immunity

Lowers Stress Hormones

Decreases Pain

Relaxes Your Muscles

Prevents Heart Disease

Strengthens Resilience

Creating Opportunities to Laugh

Watch a comedy movie, a funny TV show, or view YouTube videos

Share a funny joke or good story

Read funny books

Play with your pets

The same way that we make time every day to feed ourselves, drink water, exercise, etc. despite all that, we still must laugh every day. Laughter makes you feel better and releases healing in your body.

Yes, we all have challenges in life. If Jesus did when he was here, who are we to be exempt from challenges. The devil is always busy and as the Bible says, "The thief cometh not, but for to steal, and to kill, and to destroy: I am come that they might have life and that they might have it more abundantly." – John 10:10. You know how you make the devil mad: you keep hope alive, you have faith and trust even if it is the small size of a mustard seed in God, and you LAUGH daily!

Chapter 11

Negativity

"Let go of the people who dull your shine, poison your spirit, and bring you drama. Cancel your subscription to their issues." –Steve Maraboli

"Negativity is the enemy of creativity." — David Lynch

"There is little difference in people, but that little difference makes a big difference. The little difference is attitude. The big difference is whether it is positive or negative." — W. Clement Stone

"Fall seven times and stand up eight."–Japanese Proverb

"When the world pushes you to your knees, you're in the perfect position to pray."–Rumi

"The Meaning of ICON–I Can Overcome Negativity,"–Jennifer Lopez

There is a chemical called cortisol that is related to your hormones and stress levels. Cortisol is a chemical in your brain that tends to flow more freely and spurs negative thoughts. Your brain loves cortisol. Known as an alarm system, your brain releases the chemical cortisol as a way to warn you about an imminent danger, and, let's be honest, that's pretty helpful at times. The car in your rearview mirror is speeding up too fast; a toxic person in the office is spreading rumors about you. These experiences are common, and they trigger cortisol in your brain with a snap, which means negative thoughts come more easily than positive thoughts. The problem for a lot of us is that we develop a pattern of negativity because our brains prefer that pattern. The pump is already primed. –his is an excerpt from an article https://www.inc.com/john-brandon/science-says-there s-a-simple-reason-you-keep-thinking-negative-thoughts-all-day.html

Daily we truly must maintain control of our minds. What we allow to grow in our minds in the present and fertilize it is what our future will be like. In the same way, we must also watch the words we speak because they will also shape our future. "Death and life are in the power of the tongue: and they that love it shall eat the fruit thereof."–Proverbs 18:21. "For as he thinketh in his heart, so is he: Eat and drink, saith he to thee; but his heart is not with thee." -Proverbs 23:7. "Where the man goes, the mind follows."–Joyce Meyer.

In the same way that a car battery has a negative and positive terminal, we have the choice to live either negatively or positively. We also have the choice to speak negative or positive words and most definitely we have the choice regarding who to keep company and friendships with. Sure, we also have negative family members, but we can also control how much time we spend with them. Choice is something that God gave us from the beginning when he created Adam and Eve. God warned them about the tree of knowledge of good and evil and not to eat of it, but Eve chose to be deceived by the serpent and Adam chose to go along with Eve in eating the fruit from the tree.

Every day, we are presented with many choices, but it is up to us to choose wisely. That is why it is so critical to pray for wisdom daily. Some things we can stay away from completely. An example of this would be if you are a person who is allergic to shellfish then do not order it when dining out at a restaurant and do not buy it to cook for meals. If you do, then you know what is next, you will have to snuggle up with a bottle of Benadryl when you break out in hives. However, there are times when you do not have control over things or persons that are negative. If your co-worker is a negative person, then do not sit down and have lunch with them every day. Remember that adage that says couples married for a long time begin to look alike. "Back in 1987, scientists from the University of Michigan set out to study the phenomenon of married couples who grow to look more alike over time. (Their theory, which scientists still cite today, was that decades of shared emotions result in a closer resemblance due to similar wrinkles and expressions.)"–This is a part of an article written by JAMIE DUCHARME back on April 4, 2019, who works for Time.com. Well, the same thing applies to the company you keep. If you continuously hang around a negative person, you will pick up their habits.

Life is short and every moment counts. You do not have time to surround yourself around negativity. You need to look at the glass as half full and not half empty. Curtail negative words such as Cannot, Do not, Impossible, Unable. Instead replace them with words like: Can, Attainable, Possible, Confident, Empowered. Remember, in the Bible it says, "I can do all things through Christ which strengtheneth me." -Philippians 4:13. It is also necessary that we do not hold onto negative things that people have done to us and hurt us and keep replaying them in our minds. You are only hurting yourself. Trust me, I know firsthand. You must pray and ask God to help you to be a bigger and better person. Wrapping yourself up in negativity like the blanket that Linus carried around with him from the Charlie Brown cartoon will only detract from a life of thriving.

Pain

We have all felt some type of pain at one time or another in our lives, even infant children. Whether it is the pain of a headache, toothache, birthing a child, the death of a child, the death of a parent, the loss of a home or apartment, the loss of a job or a business, the death of a spouse, the loss of a person walking out and leaving you, not getting approved for the loan, a bankruptcy, the loss of a limb, losing out on a promotion at work, the repossession of a vehicle, a devastating medical report, the list is endless. However, whatever pain we may be enduring we must remember what God said, "Fear thou not; for I am with thee be not dismayed; for I am thy God: I will strengthen thee; yea, I will help thee; yea, I will uphold thee with the right hand of my righteousness."–Isaiah 41:10.

There was a horrific story that emerged from the news back in 2018 and an unbelievable tragedy. A family of six who lived in New Jersey was returning home from a weeklong vacation in Ocean City Maryland when their vehicle a minivan was struck by a pickup truck that crossed the median driving in the wrong direction and killed a husband and four daughters and the lone survivor was the wife and mother. The husband was 61 years old, and the daughters ranged in age from 13 to 20 years old. There are not words for this type of pain. How do you continue with such a massive loss? How do you bury five family members at the same time? How does the wife/mother go on in life and combat survivor syndrome/survivor guilt? The worst part is after a year in 2019, the driver was sentenced to one year probation and restitution with no jail time. As part of a plea deal agreement, he pleaded guilty to lesser charges: Operating a vehicle causing death and vehicular assault. The mother/wife stated, "I'll just put everything in God's hands," said Mary Rose Ballocanag. "He will give me the justice I'm always praying for." This is a woman who loves, trusts, believes, and has tremendous faith in God! What would you have done and how would you have reacted if you had to endure this type of pain?

There are a lot of buildings that are engineering marvels and for every one of them there was great study and detail that went into the construction of them. According to where a building has been erected the engineers had to consider what havoc the elements might bring. For example, in Florida, they need to consider the hurricane element and make sure the building is sturdy enough once completed. Our heavenly father, God almighty has considered all of that when he created you as to how much pain you would be able to endure. If you are still here and I'm sure you are because you are reading this, then that means you have endured 100% of the pain that has come your way. While going through the challenges, tests, trials, and pain, you thought you would never make it, but here you are still standing. You are stronger than you think. Remember what the Bible says, "Put on the whole armour of God, that ye may be able to stand against the wiles of the devil. For we wrestle not against flesh and blood, but against principalities, against powers, against the rulers of the darkness of this world, against spiritual wickedness in high places. Wherefore take unto you the whole armour of God, that ye may be able to withstand in the evil day, and having done all, to stand. Stand therefore, having your loins girt about with truth, and having on the breastplate of righteousness; And your feet shod with the preparation of the gospel of peace; Above all, taking the shield of faith, wherewith ye shall be able to quench all the fiery darts of the wicked. And take the helmet of salvation, and the sword of the Spirit, which is the word of God: Praying always with all prayer and supplication in the Spirit and watching thereunto with all perseverance and supplication for all saints." –Ephesian 6:11-18. Don't waste your pain because it is there to grow you up and develop you into the person God designed you to be when he created you. You have a bright future ahead of you.

God Is Your Pilot

The definition of a pilot is one employed to steer a ship, a person who is qualified and usually licensed to conduct a ship into and out of a port or in specified waters or a person who flies or is qualified to fly an aircraft or spacecraft. http://www.merrian-webster.com

Now I know that there are a few of you that have never ridden in a plane before or even taken a cruise. Both are truly amazing adventures. Now I realize that there have been some incidents where things did not go well with ships or planes, but you still must live your life. Remember what the Bible says, "The thief cometh not, but for to steal, and to kill, and to destroy: I am come that they might have life and that they might have it more abundantly".–John 10:10. "Charge them that are rich in this world, that they be not high-minded, nor trust in uncertain riches, but in the living God, who giveth us richly all things to enjoy".–1 Timothy 6:17. So it is very clear that God wants us to enjoy our lives, but we must remember he is the pilot. For those of you that have God as your co-pilot, and you are the pilot you need to switch seats.

In the Bible, there is the story of a prophet named Elijah. God performed quite a lot of miracles via Elijah, including resurrection, bringing fire down from the sky, and entering heaven alive "by fire." In the Bible in 1 Kings chapter 17:1-6, we see a profound example of how God is our pilot. "And Elijah the Tishbite, who was of the inhabitants of Gilead, said unto Ahab, As the Lord God of Israel liveth, before whom I stand, there shall not be dew nor rain these years, but according to my word. And the word of the Lord came unto him, saying, get thee hence, and turn thee eastward, and hide thyself by the brook Cherith, that is before Jordan. And it shall be, that thou shalt drink of the brook; and I have commanded the ravens to feed thee there. So, he went and did according unto the word of the Lord: for he went and dwelt by the brook Cherith, that is before Jordan. And the ravens brought him bread and flesh in the morning, and bread and flesh in the evening; and he drank of the brook."

So here is God's prophet who proclaimed to the people of Gilead that there would not be rain in the land for years however God told Elijah where to go to this brook that he would be able to get water from and that the ravens would bring him food day and night. How amazing is this? Not only is God commanding the ravens to bring Elijah food day and night, but he is also miraculously keeping a brook filled with water for several years when he has had Elijah proclaim there would be no rain for years. Please get this everyone. God, has you covered always even when you are being drowned by rain in the form of challenges, trials, and tests. This is a simple example of a just man who was told to go by a brook and stay there for several years. Elijah had no choice because if he wandered off, he would not have food or water to survive. The rains fell on him as well as the people in Gilead, but because he was a just man, God protected, covered, and provided for him. Remember, God is no respecter of persons if he did it for Elijah, he will do it for you as well. God is omnipresent, he is everywhere always. God is omniscient, he is aware of everything and knows everything. With a God like this, there is no way he could be anything else but a pilot. I know he is my pilot, is he yours?

Peace

"For to be carnally minded is death; but to be spiritually minded is life and peace." -Romans 8:6

Dr. Martin Luther King Jr. was all about peace. He fought his entire life for peace and equality.

Martin Luther King Jr. (born Michael King Jr.; January 15, 1929–April 4, 1968) was an American Baptist minister and activist, one of the most prominent leaders in the civil rights movement from 1955 until his assassination in 1968. An African American church leader and the son of early civil rights activist and minister Martin Luther King Sr., King advanced civil rights for people of color in the United States through nonviolence and civil disobedience. Inspired by his Christian beliefs and the nonviolent activism of Mahatma Gandhi, he led targeted, nonviolent resistance against Jim Crow laws and other forms of discrimination. - https://en.wikipedia.org/wiki/Martin_Luther_King_Jr.

Dr. King preached a sermon on March 18, 1956, in Montgomery Alabama titled ""When Peace Becomes Obnoxious". Part of the speech goes as follows, "A few weeks ago, a federal judge handed down an edict, which stated in substance that the university of Alabama could no longer deny admission to persons because of their race. With the handing down of this decision, a brave young lady by the name of Autherine Lucy was accepted as the first Negro student to be admitted in the history of the university of Alabama. This was a great moment and a great decision. But with the announcement of this decision, the vanguards of the old order began to emerge. The forces of evil began to congeal. As soon as Autherine Lucy walked on the campus, a group of spoiled students lead by Leonard Wilson and a vicious group of criminals began threatening her on every hand. Crosses were burned. Eggs and bricks were thrown at her. The mob even jumped on top of the car in which she was riding. Finally, the president and trustees of the university of Alabama asked Autherine to leave for her own safety and the safety of the university. The next day after Autherine was dismissed the paper came out with this headline: "Things are quiet in Tuscaloosa today. There is peace on the campus of the university of Alabama." Yes, things were quiet in Tuscaloosa. Yes, there was peace on the campus, but it was peace at a great price. It was peace that had been purchased at the exorbitant price of an inept trustee board succumbing to the whims and caprice of a vicious mob. It was peace that had been purchased at the price of allowing mobocracy to reign supreme over democracy. It was peace that had been purchased at the price of the capitulating to the forces of darkness. This is the type of peace that all men of goodwill hate. It is the type of peace that is obnoxious. It is the type of peace that stinks in the nostrils of the almighty God. - https://kinginstitute.stanford.edu/king-papers/documents/when-peace -becomes-obnoxious

What does the word peace mean? The dictionary definition states a state of tranquility or quiet. We should strive for peace in all situations, such as: War - Then Jesus said to him, "Put your sword back into its place. For all who take the sword will perish by the sword. -Matthew 26:52. Love - Charity suffereth long and is kind; charity envieth not; charity vaunteth not itself, is not puffed up, Doth not behave itself unseemly, seeketh not her own, is not easily provoked, thinketh no evil; Rejoiceth not in iniquity, but rejoiceth in the truth; Beareth all things, believeth all things, hopeth all things, endureth all things. Charity never faileth: but whether there be prophecies, they shall fail; whether there be tongues, they shall cease; whether there be knowledge, it shall vanish away." -1 Corinthians 4-8. Enemies - "But I say to you who hear, love your enemies, do good to those who hate you, bless those who curse you, pray for those who abuse you. To one who strikes you on the cheek, offer the other also, and from one who takes away your cloak do not withhold your tunic either. Give to everyone who begs from you, and from one who takes away your goods do not demand them back. And as you wish that others would do to you, do so to them." -Luke 6:27-31.

So, what can we do on a daily spiritual basis to instill peace? Let's look at an acronym for peace and start there.

P = Profess - Everyone of us has had a godly experience of some sort that we know human flesh was incapable of making that situation even happen or happen as swiftly as it did. In my situation, it was to quit smoking instantly after 20 years of smoking every day with no patches, smokeless cigarettes, or anything at all. Now that was a miracle and I've never gone back. Whatever your experience is profess it to the world what God has done for you.

E = Educate - Talk and teach others about how wonderful it is to be a child of God. "For God so loved the world, that he gave his only begotten Son, that whosoever believeth in him should not perish, but have everlasting life." -John 3:16. He that spared not his own Son, but delivered him up for us all, how shall he not with him also freely give us all things? -Romans 8:32

A = Appreciate - We all need to show gratitude to God for all that he has done for us daily. We have all heard the phrase " the little things mean so much", well that is true. Be grateful for things you never think about. Are you able to walk, talk, drive, see, hear, go to the bathroom by yourself without the assistance of a wheelchair or human being? If so, then you are already out of the starting gate doing well and we all know how that turned out for "Justify" the horse racing world's latest triple crown winner.

C = Charity - In our world nowadays, there are multitudes of companies asking for charity. However, you must be selective and careful as to who you choose to help, but you are required by God to assist. "For ye have the poor always with you; but me ye have not always." -Matthew 26:11. "A good man sheweth favour, and lendeth: he will guide his affairs with discretion. Surely, he shall not be moved forever: the righteous shall be in everlasting remembrance. He shall not be afraid of evil tidings: his heart is fixed, trusting in the Lord. His heart is established, he shall not be afraid, until he sees his desire upon his enemies. He hath dispersed, he hath given to the poor; his righteousness endureth for ever; his horn shall be exalted with honour." -Psalms 112: 5-9

E = Empathy - We have all also heard the phrase "walk a mile in my shoes" but would we really want to in some circumstances. There is a reason why God gave us two ears and one mouth so we can listen and share other people's feelings, experiences, and emotions. "Before you criticize someone, you should walk a mile in their shoes. That way when you criticize them, you are a mile away from them and you have their shoes." - Jack Handey.

God requires us to live a peaceful life. He sent his son Jesus to die on the cross so we could all live abundant lives. You cannot live an abundant life when you are always worried, stressed out, sitting on pins and needles. Give it all to God and trust in his plan for your life.

Chapter 12

If You're Going Through Hell Keep Going

Your boss asks you to work late. You miss your child's school play. Your car breaks down on your way to work and needs to be towed. You forget to transfer funds to cover your cell phone bill and so the payment defaults and they suspend your service. The regular coffee shop that serves you your coffee every day makes the wrong order but, you need it anyway because you are making a presentation this morning at work, and you need the pick me up. As you go through the revolving door of your office building, it jams and once it rotates again, it jolts and spills coffee all over your business suit. You leave work early and go home to cook a special dinner for your child as an apology for missing the school play and the oven catches on fire and blows up.

Winston Churchill said, "If You're Going Through Hell Keep Going,"

All of us have had days like this in our lives. You can either give up and think life is against you or you can do like hockey players do when they get knocked down on the ice. They keep getting up time and time again. When faced with a challenge, we can either wilt or rise above.

I live in the state of Florida and recently NASA has encountered some days of hell with the launches they had planned. They have had to postpone the Artemis rocket launches twice already. They have three missions, and they are planning to get the first one corrected and ready for launch on September 27, 2022. Well, what does this mean? With the delays, this causes cost overruns. "The original cost for the S-L-S, or "Space Launch System," which includes the rocket and boosters that propel the Orion capsule into space, has grown from $10 billion to $20 billion. Each successful launch will cost about $4.1 billion. NASA's inspector general expects the overall Artemis program to reach $93 billion by the time the first astronauts return to the surface of the moon, targeted for 2025." - https://www.voanews.com/a/despite-cost-overruns-and-delays-nasa-hopes-to-launch-artemis-1-this-year-/6746292.html. – This except is from Kane Farabaugh, who is the Midwest Correspondent for Voice of America, where since 2008 he has established Voice of America's presence in the heartland of America.

The second issue with the delays is that when there is a launch, people come out to witness it firsthand and, for those individuals, it is also costly with fuel for their vehicles, possibly hotel expenses, etc.

Many biblical figures had tough days as well.

Job - lost his children, his wealth, his health, his livestock, and his crops. Job suffered tremendously but, in the end, God restored Job twice his original loss.

David - was anointed to be king by God, but for several years of his life, he had to run for his life from King Saul. Eventually, David became Israel's second and greatest king.

Mary - was promised to Joseph in marriage at an early age. Mary's claim of virginity caused her much stress once she was carrying the baby, Jesus. People looked at her differently, whispered, snickered, and stared at her. Mary, however, became the mother of mothers and one of the most prolific persons in the bible.

Joseph - was sold into Egyptian slavery by his brothers. After he earned his master's trust, the lies of the master's wife landed Joseph in prison. Joseph could interpret dreams and one day he interpreted a dream for someone who was also imprisoned and once released, this man forgot his promise to Joseph to speak to the master to sing Joseph's praises and promptly forgot about his promise for two years. When the master had a troubling dream, Joseph was remembered and was called before the master to interpret the dream. Once Joseph interpreted the dream for the master, they released him from prison, and he became second in command behind the master. Joseph waited 13 years for his dream to come true.

There are a tremendous number of biblical figures that endured tough times but persevered and were rewarded by God. So, when you have those days that appear ready to destroy you, remember the famous words of Winston Churchill, "When you're going through hell, keep going."

Greatness Requires Discomfort

If you want to do great things in life and especially great things for God, there is going to be some discomfort. Life is just not wine and roses and when he was here over 2,000 years ago, Jesus had to go through a lot of discomfort.

In the Bible, the Apostle Paul, who wrote 14 books in the New Testament, had to go through a lot of discomfort. He endured a lot of challenges because of the work he had in front of him he needed to do where Jesus was concerned. Paul said, "And now, behold, I go bound in the spirit unto Jerusalem, not knowing the things that shall befall me there: Save that the Holy Ghost witnesseth in every city, saying that bonds and afflictions abide me. But none of these things move me, neither count I my life dear unto myself, so that I might finish my course with joy, and the ministry, which I have received of the Lord Jesus, to testify the gospel of the grace of God." -Acts 20:22-24.

Mary, the mother of Jesus, also had to encounter a great deal of discomfort. Can you just imagine how she was talked about, ridiculed, and disowned by friends and family once they knew she was pregnant and was not married? Back in those days, when something of this magnitude came to light, they stoned the woman to death! Can you imagine being a fly on the wall and listening to her explaining to Joseph, her fiancé, that she is pregnant but was never with a man and the pregnancy is from The Holy Spirit?

People from every caliber of life who have accomplished impressive feats have had to endure discomfort. Whether you are an actor, politician, singer, news reporter, pastor, athlete or a host or many other industry types.

One of the greatest pitchers ever to step on a baseball mound was Jim Abbott. What made Jim Abbott so successful, he was born without a right hand. He played for the California Angels, New York Yankees, Chicago White Sox, and Milwaukee Brewers, from 1989 to 1999. When preparing to pitch the ball, Abbott would rest his glove on the end of his right forearm. After releasing the ball, he would quickly slip his hand into the glove, usually in time to field any balls that a two-handed pitcher would be able to field. Then he would secure the glove between his right forearm and torso, slip his hand out of the glove, and remove the ball from the glove, usually in time to throw out the runner at first or sometimes even start a double play. At all levels, teams tried to exploit his fielding disadvantage by repeatedly bunting to him. His disability inspired him to work harder than most. "As a kid I really wanted to fit in," Abbott says on his website about growing up with a disability. "Sports became a way for me to gain acceptance. I think this fueled my desire to succeed. I truly believe that difficult times and disappointments can push us to find abilities and strengths we wouldn't know existed without the experience of struggle." - https://en.wikipe dia.org/wiki/Jim_Abbott. Do you think it was ever uncomfortable for him when he stepped on the mound or when he was in practice? Of course, he dealt with discomfort, but he pushed through it and had a tremendous career and became a role model for many others. Since his retirement, he is currently a motivational speaker.

We all have been given an assignment to complete here on earth. God has gifted each one of us with what we need to accomplish that task. No matter how much rain falls on you, just keep in mind when the three Hebrew children were tossed in the fiery furnace that when the king looked, he saw a fourth man in the fire with them that was God.

Stepping Out Of Your Comfort Zone

We all have a comfort zone where we feel at peace, relaxed, there are no struggles, no challenges. It is like the Peanuts cartoon figure Linus with his blanket. He took it with him everywhere and it just made him feel safe and comfortable. Or maybe it's a cold winter morning and you feel so warm and cozy under the covers and you just don't want to move to start your day. However, if you are going to do great things for God, you are going to have to step out of your comfort zone.

God will not allow you to just coast through life. You must have those challenges, you must be stretched, you must be on the potter's wheel. God is faithful to bless you if you will leave fear behind or do it afraid and follow what God asks you to do. God is always ordering your steps, and he has a glorious future in store for you. So, step out of your comfort zone and you will see that God means what he says," Now unto him that is able to do exceeding abundantly above all that we ask or think, according to the power that worketh in us," –Ephesians 3:20. This is not something that is just happening to present-day people, it happened to biblical people as well. Abraham was stretched and had to step out of his comfort zone.

"Now the Lord had said unto Abram, Get thee out of thy country, and from thy kindred, and from thy father's house, unto a land that I will shew thee: And I will make of thee a great nation, and I will bless thee, and make thy name great; and thou shalt be a blessing: And I will bless them that bless thee, and curse him that curseth thee: and in thee shall all families of the earth be blessed. So Abram departed, as the Lord had spoken unto him; and Lot went with him: and Abram was seventy and five years old when he departed out of Haran And Abram took Sarai his wife, and Lot his brother's son, and all their substance that they had gathered, and the souls that they had gotten in Haran; and they went forth to go into the land of Canaan; and into the land of Canaan they came."–Genesis 12:1-5.

"Don't let fear make your decisions for you." -Annette White

"I'm not telling you it's going to be easy; I'm telling you it's going to b worth it." -Anonymous.

"The comfort zone is nothing else but a graveyard for your dreams & ideas." -Anonymous

"You can choose courage, or you can choose comfort. You cannot have both." -Brene Brown

"The hardest thing to do is leaving your comfort zone. But you have to let go of the life you're familiar with and take the risk to live the life you dream about." -T. Arigo

"The only thing that is stopping you from where you are to where you want to go is your comfort zone." -Dhaval Gaudier

"A ship is always safe at the shore-but that is not what it is built for." -Albert Einstein

Don't allow the distractions of life that Satan sends your way to prevent you from the brilliant future and destiny God has arranged for you. No amount of rain will stop you from what God has arranged for you. If you want to do great things in life, you need to get away from the normal and step into the abnormal. Even if you are feeling fearful, do it anyway. FEAR is just "False Evidence Appearing Real", and this stops most people from becoming great.

The Battle Is Not Yours It's The Lords

We all face battles in life. Some are small and others are overwhelming. Battles come in all forms, shapes, and sizes. Whether it is a health battle, financial, job related, family or friends, or a host of other types. What we must remember is that God is our vindicator, and the battle belongs to him. What we are supposed to do is leave it to God and get in prayer and praise and worship position.

"And he said, hearken ye, all Judah, and ye inhabitants of Jerusalem, and thou king Jehoshaphat, thus saith the Lord unto you, be not afraid nor dismayed by reason of this great multitude; for the battle is not yours, but God's. Tomorrow go ye down against them: behold, they come up by the cliff of Ziz; and ye shall find them at the end of the brook, before the wilderness of Jeruel. Ye shall not need to fight in this battle: set yourselves, stand ye still, and see the salvation of the Lord with you, O Judah and Jerusalem: fear not, nor be dismayed; tomorrow go out against them: for the Lord will be with you." –2 Chronicles 20:15-17. Notice the words that are used in this passage: You will not need to fight. Position yourself.

Stand still and see. Do not fear. There are a lot of action words here, but it's clearly conveyed that all God's people must do is to be obedient and submissive to God and He will do the rest.

In the book of Judges, Chapter 7, there was a man named Gideon, who had an army of 32,000 men and was about to wage war on the Midianites. The Midianites were the people whose hands the children of Israel were delivered for seven years by the Lord because Israel did evil in the Lord's sight. When the Lord was ready to destroy the Midianties, he sent an angel who appeared unto Gideon and said, "The Lord is with thee, thou mighty man of valor."

Now, as Gideon was prepared to wage war, the Lord wasn't pleased with the company of men Gideon had. And the Lord said unto Gideon, "The people that are with thee are too many for me to give the Midianites into their hands, lest Israel vaunt themselves against me, saying, 'Mine own hand hath saved me.' And so, as you read on further, you will see that Gideon cut down his company of men from 32,000 to 10,000. God again spoke to Gideon and said that the men he had with him were still too many." Verse 4 reads: "And the Lord said unto Gideon, "The people are yet too many; bring them down to the water, and I will try them for thee there; and it shall be that of whom I say unto thee,,"This shall not go with thee, the same shall not go." As you continue to read on among verses 5-8, God explained to Gideon what formula he would use to lessen his troop. As you can clearly see, God will not share his glory with any man. He cut the troop down to 300 men. Remember, back in verse 2, where God says,,"Less the men say mine own hand hath saved me." And so, the Lord delivered the Midianites into the hand of Gideon and his downsized army of 300 men. "And it came to pass the same night that the Lord said unto him, 'Arise, get thee down unto the host; for I have delivered it into thine hand.'" God used a very unusual way to deliver the Midianites into the hand of Gideon and his army, you can read the entire story of Gideon in the Bible in Judges 6:11–Judges 8.

We all know the classic movie by director Cecil B. DeMille "The Ten Commandments" and how Pharaoh's army was destroyed in the Red Sea. "And the Lord said unto Moses, stretch out thine hand over the sea, that the waters may come again upon the Egyptians, upon their chariots, and upon their horsemen.

And Moses stretched forth his hand over the sea, and the sea returned to his strength when the morning appeared, and the Egyptians fled against it, and the Lord overthrew the Egyptians in the midst of the sea. And the waters returned and covered the chariots, and the horsemen, and all the host of Pharaoh that came into the sea after them; there remained not so much as one of them. But the children of Israel walked upon dry land in the midst of the sea, and the waters were a wall unto them on their right hand, and on their left. Thus, the Lord saved Israel that day out of the hand of the Egyptians; and Israel saw the Egyptians dead upon the seashore." –Exodus 14:26-30.

God is an all-powerful, almighty, exceptional Lord. God is a Lord of justice and will never leave you or forsake you ever. The Almighty is a conqueror. Test your faith. What problem do you currently have that needs to be battled? Are you going through a battle with an employer, spouse, family member, friend, or even your children? You can't change them, only God can. Remember, The Battle Is Not Yours - It's the Lords.

Stop The Excuses

What is the opposite of stop the excuses? It is obedience. Obedient - submissive to the restraint or command of authority: willing to obey. - https://www.merriam-webster.com/dictionary/obedient

Are you obedient and submissive to God? Well, if you are, miracles will happen. Every day we have the choice whether to be obedient to many things. If you are a driver, you must be obedient to the traffic signs and signals. If you are an employee, you need to be obedient to your superiors or else you will be fired. There are many other examples, but the biggest one of all is to be obedient to God.

Disciple Simon Peter

"After these things Jesus shewed himself again to the disciples at the sea of Tiberias; and on this wise shewed he himself. There was together Simon Peter, and Thomas called Didymus, and Nathanael of Cana in Galilee, and the sons of Zebedee, and two others of his disciples. Simon Peter saith unto them, I go a fishing. They say unto him, we also go with thee. They went forth and entered into a ship immediately; and that night they caught nothing. But when the morning was now come, Jesus stood on the shore: but the disciples knew not that it was Jesus. Then Jesus saith unto them, Children, have ye any meat? They answered him, No. And he said unto them, Cast the net on the right side of the ship, and ye shall find. They cast therefore, and now they were not able to draw it for the multitude of fishes. Therefore, that disciple whom Jesus loved saith unto Peter, it is the Lord. Now when Simon Peter heard that it was the Lord, he girt his fisher's coat unto him, (for he was naked,) and did cast himself into the sea. And the other disciples came in a little ship; (for they were not far from land, but as it were two hundred cubits,) dragging the net with fishes. As soon then as they were come to land, they saw a fire of coals there, and fish laid thereon, and bread. Jesus saith unto them, bring of the fish which ye have now caught. Simon Peter went up, and drew the net to land full of great fishes, an hundred and fifty and three: and for all there were so many, yet was not the net broken." –John 21:1-11.

Now the above example clearly shows how obedience pays off. Jesus instructed the disciples to not only cast their nets, but that they must cast them on the right side of the ship. If they didn't obey and cast the nets on the left side of the ship, they would never have gotten any fish.

Tribute Money

"And when they were come to Capernaum, they that received tribute money came to Peter, and said, Doth not your master pay tribute? He saith, yes. And when he was come into the house, Jesus prevented him, saying, what thinkest thou, Simon? Of whom do the kings of the earth take custom or tribute? Of their own children, or of strangers? Peter saith unto him, Of strangers. Jesus saith unto him, then are the children free. Notwithstanding, lest we should offend them, go thou to the sea, and cast an hook, and take up the fish that first cometh up; and when thou hast opened his mouth, thou shalt find a piece of money: that take, and give unto them for me and thee." –Matthew 17:24-27. What was the obedience factor here? Jesus told Peter to take up the first fish. If Peter had decided to wait for a different fish, then the tax money would not have been received to pay tribute.

Nick Vujicic

There is a man by the name of Nick Vujicic, who is an Australian American Christian Evangelist and motivational speaker. What makes Nick so unique is that he was born with tetra-amelia syndrome, a rare disorder characterised by the absence of arms and legs. Originally, the toes of one of his feet were fused. An operation was performed to separate the toes so that he can use them as fingers to grab. He refers to it as his chicken drumstick. - https://en.wikipedia.org/wiki/Nick_Vujicic

I had the pleasure of seeing him live and in person several years ago when he came to speak at my church. It was astounding to see how he handled a computer tablet with his foot. He can type 43 words per minute with his foot. In 2012, he married his wife Kanae and they have four children. He is also the founder and CEO of the non-profit ministry Life Without Limbs. His website says OBSTACLES = OPPORTUNITY. https://nickvujicic.com/

So just to be blunt, what plausible excuse can you come up with now not to live the life God gave you and to complete your assignment he gave you? STOP THE EXCUSES!!!!!!!!!!!!!!!!!!!!!!!!!!!!!

Chapter 13

Jesus Is Not A Hobby

Most of us have some type of hobby whether it is photography, gardening, scrapbooking, video playing, painting, playing chess, or a host of others. However, when you have a hobby, that is something that you do two, maybe three times a week. That is not the way you can manage where God is concerned. God desires for you to have an intimate relationship with him daily. That is what he created us for, to be in constant communication and fellowship with him.

God is not something that you can just place in a jewelry box or drawer and pull out whenever you feel like it. It is not just going to church on Sundays. You need to be reading and studying the word. You need to be thanking him for all the blessings he has provided you with daily. Yes, God does provide blessings daily the word says so, "Blessed be the Lord, who daily loadeth us with benefits, even the God of our salvation. Selah."–Psalms 68:19.

Having an intimate relationship with God requires you to be diligent and engrossed in what you're doing. When you are diligent that is not something that goes on two or three times a week. You go out to work at least four times a week if you are on a ten-hour schedule where you work four days and are off three. So, if God gives you the strength to work like that, why don't you have time for him?

Life gets in the way...I'm so busy I can't take on another thing... I would love to but I'm so tired.

How does your day breakdown?

Shower - 10 minutes

Brush Teeth - 2 to 3 minutes

Shave - 5 to 8 minutes

Get Dressed - 15 minutes

Walk the dog - 15 minutes

Get the children dressed - 20 minutes

Give the children breakfast - 30 minutes

Drink a cup of coffee - 10-15 minutes

Eat breakfast - 7-20 minutes

Drop the children off at school - 20 minutes

Drive to the office to work - 10 to 45 minutes

Workout/Exercise - 30 to 60 minutes

Grocery Shopping - 45 to 60 minutes

Business Meeting at the office - 60 to 120 minutes

Eat lunch - 25 minutes

Talk with friends - 45 minutes/include texting 1-3 hours

Pay Bills on the Internet - 15 minutes

Pick up the children from school - 30 minutes

Help children with their homework - 60 minutes

Prepare dinner - 30 to 75 minutes

Drive back home from work - 10 to 45 minutes

Eat dinner as a family - 20 to 40 minutes

Feed the dog/cat/pet - 5 minutes

Talk & spend time with spouse 20 to 40 minutes

Put the children to bed - 10-15 minutes

Clean the cat litter pan or pet - 15 minutes

Work on presentation for work - 45 to 90 minutes

Watch TV - 30-120 minutes

Daily Work–8 hours

If you calculate all the above minutes on the lower side of the scale, that amounts to 18 hours and 39 minutes. Well, that leaves less than 6 hours of sleep. No wonder we don't get the proper rest for our bodies, but we expect them to just keep going strong like an energizer bunny. Remember what the Bible says, "What? know ye not that your body is the temple of the Holy Ghost, which is in you, which ye have of God, and ye are not your own? For ye are bought with a price: therefore, glorify God in your body, and in your spirit, which are God's." -1 Corinthians 6:19-20. This Bible verse does not just imply using drugs or continuous unhealthy eating, it also implies to making sure your body gets the correct amount of rest.

However, what I want you to see here is that the above schedule did not include any time spent with God. Well, let's just ponder this for a moment. If GOD gives you the grace daily to meet all these obligations and more and makes sure you have use of all your five senses and mobility in your limbs to perform these tasks, then don't you think a simple prayer and praise and gratitude should be acknowledged towards him every day before you start your day? No wonder the rain falls on the just and the unjust.

The Essence Of Prayer

Essence - the most significant element, quality, or aspect of a thing or person the essence of the issue. https://www.merriam-webster.com/dictionary/essence

Prayer - an address (such as a petition) to God or a god in word or thought; something prayed for. https://www.merriam-webster.com/dictionary/prayer

Your prayer life needs to be simple. "But thou, when thou prayest, enter into thy closet, and when thou hast shut thy door, pray to thy Father which is in secret; and thy Father which seeth in secret shall reward thee openly. But when ye pray, use not vain repetitions, as the heathen do: for they think that they shall be heard for their much speaking. Be not ye, therefore, like unto them: for your father knoweth what things ye have need of before ye ask him. After this manner, therefore, pray ye: Our Father which art in heaven, hallowed be thy name. Thy kingdom come, thy will be done on earth, as it is in heaven. Give us this day our daily bread. And forgive us our debts, as we forgive our debtors. And lead us not into temptation but deliver us from evil: For thine is the kingdom, and the power, and the glory, forever. Amen." –Matthew 6:6-13. This is a very simple prayer that Jesus gave us to pray.

The Bible gives us an excellent example of someone who took his prayer life seriously. "Daniel always prayed to God three times every day. Three times every day, he bowed down on his knees to pray and praise God. Even though Daniel heard about the new law, he still went to his house to pray. He went up to the upper room of his house and opened the windows that faced toward Jerusalem. Then Daniel bowed down on his knees and prayed just as he always had done ." –Daniel 6:10. King Darius loved Daniel and intended to make him in charge of the entire kingdom and, of course, the other men became jealous and decided they needed to come up with a plot to have the king dislike Daniel. Well, as you know, the story went on to say they told the king that no one should worship anyone except him for the next 30 days and if they didn't follow orders, they were to be thrown in the lion's den.

As the Bible states in the verse above, Daniel not only continued to pray to God, but he did so three times a day. Well, of course, this hurt the king, and he had no choice but to throw him in the lion's den. However, the king was worried all night until in the morning he rushed to the lion's den and called out Daniel's name and he came forth unharmed. Well, you know the old saying when you dig a ditch, dig two or the Bible verse, "Whoso diggeth a pit shall fall therein: and he that rolleth a stone, it will return upon him." –Proverbs 26:27. So, of course, King Darius promptly had the other men and their families thrown in the lion's den and the lions tore them to shreds. Therefore, we don't have to get back at people who hurt us because God is our vindicator, and he will repay. The Bible says so, "Dearly beloved, avenge not yourselves, but rather give place unto wrath: for it is written, Vengeance is mine; I will repay, saith the Lord." –Romans 12:19.

However, what I really wanted you to see is that God did not keep Daniel from being placed in the lion's den, but he covered and protected and spared his life because he was a just man. So yes, the rain did fall on Daniel, but he came through the situation victoriously!

It's Just A Test–Prayer Is The Answer

The word test seems to abound. There are several types of tests. You have an assessment test you take in school, driving test, health check test, eye examination test, dental exam tests. Etc. These are tests that we are all familiar with and must take at one time or another in our lives. However, are you aware that God tests us as well? God tests us to prove our faith. God will allow a certain number of trials and tribulations to come our way in this life, however, he will also use some of these trials as a way of testing all of us out from time to time to see if we have learned what He has been teaching us. He rarely, if ever, announces them ahead of time. They just come.

From time-to-time God will place us in uncomfortable situations that put us under pressure to show what our true character is. "The Lord trieth the righteous: but the wicked and him that loveth violence his soul hateth." –Psalm 11:5.

A while back, I was introduced to the Book of James that has a very profound set of verses that tell us to expect tests and that we should delight in them. "My brethren, count it all joy when ye fall into diver's temptations, Knowing this, that the trying of your faith worketh patience. But let patience have her perfect work, that ye may be perfect and entire, wanting nothing." –James 1:2-4. Now, for those of you that have a type-A personality like myself, this was not something I wanted to read or hear. I am sure no one wants to be joyful when things are not going their way. I am very sure patience is the last thing on anybody's mind when things are not going smoothly. We want it fixed and done like yesterday! When we are in an uncomfortable situation and our flesh is not enjoying it, we want it fixed immediately. However, that is not the way God works. According to him, tests are beneficial. Tests are God's way of moving us out of our comfort zones. "Comfort is the enemy of progress."–The Greatest Showman Movie quote.

There are several types of tests but here are some of the top ones.

The People Test–Do you place your faith in people? People are human and frail, just like yourself. They may be there for you for a season, but eventually, God will remove them, so you can place your faith where it truly belongs, which is in God. "That your faith should not stand in the wisdom of men but in the power of God." –1 Corinthians 2:5.

The Pressure Test–When all hell is breaking loose, and things are tumultuous, will you depend on yourself or depend on God? "And call upon me in the day of trouble: I will deliver thee, and thou shalt glorify me." –Psalm 50:15.

The Faith Test–Do you have faith in God, or do you operate from your feelings more? Noah operated in faith when God spoke to him and advised him to build an ark because the end of all flesh was coming because God was going to flood the earth and destroy all mankind and animals and beasts. "Thus, did Noah; according to all that God commanded him, so did he." You can read the entire story in Genesis 6-8.

The Patience Test–This is one of the hardest tests of all, especially if you are a type-A personality. This is where you have done everything you have been asked to do, but now God is going to ask you to just sit and wait for the big breakthrough to occur. This is the position Moses was in after Pharaoh finally released the people of Israel. They had traveled and walked so long, and the promise land was on the other side of the Red Sea. Once they reached the Red Sea, God made Moses and the people of Israel wait before he parted it. The people started to complain to Moses why didn't you just leave us in Egypt with Pharaoh instead of bringing us out here to die in the wilderness and in the sea. God did eventually part the Red Sea, and the people crossed over to the other side and Pharaoh's army was killed in the sea when God brought the waters back together.

The Obedience Test–There is one test in the Bible that brings tears to your eyes and fills you with joy at the same time. This is the story of Abraham and his son Isaac. God asked Abraham to put his son Isaac on an altar and then asked him to take a knife and kill his own son. As we all know, Abraham went as far as to tie his son down to the altar and had the knife in his hand ready to strike down on him to take his life, when suddenly God sends an angel down in the nick of time to stop him. Would you be obedient to God to this length?

Most tests that God puts you through are not this daunting. Tests are more in the realm of do you trust God, or do you worry? Do you have patience in a traffic jam or in line at the supermarket? Do you throw your hands in the air and give up as soon as you are disappointed? Where would we all be if Thomas Edison just gave up and didn't pass the test?

Thomas Edison Quotes:

"Our greatest weakness lies in giving up. The most certain way to succeed is always to try just one more time."

"Genius is one percent inspiration and ninety-nine percent perspiration."

"I have not failed. I've just found 10,000 ways that won't work."

"Many of life's failures are people who did not realize how close they were to success when they gave up."

What we all need to do while we are waiting for our breakthrough is pray. However, the type of prayers you should say is to ask God to change you. God is interested in refining you and changing you, and he does this through these tests. If your weakness is patience, then God will see that you are always in the wrong line in the supermarket. Or you always get caught up in traffic just to test your patience. The thing about tests is that God will allow you to take them repeatedly until you pass them. Keep praying even though it seems like God went on vacation. God knows exactly where you are in life. Pay attention to the areas you are being tested in. It will make you more aware once God tests you. When you become familiar with the same patterns, you will realize it is just a test. Pass it and move on. The faster you do, the faster God will open the skies and rain down, exceeding and abundant blessing on your life and bring you into your divine destiny.

Keep Speaking Victory

We all are going to come to a point in our lives where we encounter challenges. Whether that be health challenges, financial challenges, marital challenges, employment challenges or challenges of other sorts. When we reach this point, it is critical that we keep always speaking victory. It is very important that you remember that your words and thoughts create your destiny.

In the Bible, there was a man named Caleb who, along with Joshua, went with ten other men that Moses sent to spy on the land of Canaan. Well, Caleb, along with Joshua, came back and informed Moses that the people in the land were giants but that we could overtake them and take the land. The other ten spies, however, cowered and stated that the men in Canaan were too big, and we could never defeat them. The children of Israel became fearful and spoke a lot of negative things and listened to the ten men and refused to go in and take the land.

Caleb was forty years old when Moses sent him and Joshua and the other ten spies. Suffice it to say, only Caleb and Joshua made it into the promise land out of the two million Israelites from the older generation. When Caleb was 85 years old, he went to Joshua, who was now the man in charge after Moses passed away and said, "I am just as strong now as I was when I was forty. Give me this mountain and I will conquer it." Caleb was asking for the mountain side of Hebron and Joshua obliged and gave it to him. Why did he get what he was seeking forty-five years earlier? Caleb kept speaking victory. He believed he could conquer, and he did.

Now, for those of you that are baseball fans, you will understand completely the example I am about to state. If you are not a baseball fan or maybe not a sports fan at all, just follow along you will get the gist of what I am saying. There is a player by the name of Wynton Bernard who has been playing in the minor leagues for a decade. Yes, I said a decade 10 years ago. He finally received the call to play in a Major League Baseball game August 2022 and it became a magical night. He stepped up to the plate, got a hit and because of his speed, he was called safe at first base by the home plate umpire. The pitcher on the mound was so deep in thought about the next player at home plate that he forgot about Wynton, who was on first base and with Wynton's speed, he was able to steal second base and was called safe. The player who was at home plate also got a hit and because of Wynton's speed, he was able to run the bases and come all the way around from second base to home plate and score. Well, what he did by scoring broke the tie between the two baseball teams, and eventually, Wynton's team was able to hold on and win the game. So, Wynton became the MVP (Most Valuable Player) of the game. How outstanding was that? Why did that happen for him because he stayed in the game for ten years in the minors until his appointed time came and because he kept speaking victory over his life.

Chapter 14

Victim Mentality

Victim - one that is acted on and usually adversely affected by a force or agent; one that is subjected to oppression, hardship, or mistreatment. https://www.merriam-webster.com/dictionary/victim

Mentality - mode or way of thought; outlookhttps://www.merriam-webster.com/dictionary/mentality.

Drag your thoughts away from your troubles... by the ears, by the heels, or any other way you can manage it. – Mark Twain

As I am writing this, I am reflecting on times that I was fighting thoughts of victim mentality myself. Every talented writer knows personal stories are vital to them being successful. Don't be afraid to be open and vulnerable! Write about your challenging times and how you overcame them or are overcoming them. This is a concept I am very familiar with as I have had to do this, and it has brought me remarkable success as I have been one of 50 finalists for the "50 Great Writers You Should Be Reading" book for 2015, 2016, 2017, & 2018 for The Author Show. I was also a nominee for The Top Female Author for 2017. I was honored & humbled when I won the award in 2018 for Top Female Author in the categories of Religion/Philosophy/Spirituality. I have also been blessed to have received 5

Star reviews for my past two books from Readers Favorite as well as #1 Best-Selling Author for my past two books.

I have written a previous blog titled "Abase and Abounding" when we go through highs and lows in our lives. There are also times when we sometimes feel like victims and that is the thought process in our minds. Thoughts run through our minds like life is not fair, I never get the good breaks, why do I always end up with the short end of the stick, it's just another day everything is still the same, Is God on vacation, did he forget about me? We are all guided by our minds. We become what we think about. When we feel like we have entered the stage of victim mentality, we must break that thought process immediately, and the quickest way is to start a gratitude process.

Every day, we should make a list of at least 10 things we should be grateful for before we start our day. You can write it on an index card, do a word document, or use the memo pad on your phone and create the list. When we send positive, grateful thoughts through our mind, we don't have time to have a negative thought process, which would include having a victim mentality. "The world as we have created it is a process of our thinking. It cannot be changed without changing our thinking." –Albert Einstein.

When we do, we need to be grateful for the smaller things when we are given bigger things. We need to be grateful for the food we eat, the water we drink, the choices we have for cellular services, cable services, supermarkets to shop at, etc., the things nature offers such as planet earth, air, and the sun. –"I started out giving thanks for small things, and the more thankful I became, the more my bounty increased. That's because what you focus on expands, and when you focus on the goodness in your life, you create more of it. Opportunities, relationships, even money flowed my way when I learned to be grateful no matter what happened in my life."–Oprah Winfrey.

So, whenever you are having your difficulties and highs and lows and feel you are slipping into a victim mentality mode, remember you must allow a power greater than you to take care of the how. "For I know the plans I have for you," declares the Lord, "plans to prosper you and not to harm you, plans to give you hope and a future." - Jeremiah 29:11.

Feelings Vs Faith

Feelings–an emotional state or reaction.https://www.merriam-webster.com/dictionary/feelings

Faith -something that is believed, especially with strong conviction, belief and trust in and loyalty to God. https://www.merriam-webster.com/dictionary/faith

We are created as emotional beings. Feelings aren't wrong, but a believer's life is meant to be based on faith, not on feelings. Feelings have a prominent place in our lives, but we can't use them to guide our lives. Feelings come and go and are unreliable guides to the truth and what is right. Whenever we walk by feelings rather than faith, we fail. Many people just glide through life, running on emotion. Christ had feelings and emotions and he didn't hide them. Jesus wept when he came to the grave of Lazarus.

They say that anger weakens the liver, grief weakens the lungs, worry weakens the stomach, stress weakens the heart and brain, and fear fails the kidneys. So where do these things come from that weaken our systems? Disturbances from our spouse, family members, place of employment, the news media, etc. These are all examples of feelings. Knowing about God and his will and obediently following him are the basics of a believer's discipleship. Faith has nothing to do with feelings. Faith rests on the absolute word of God.

In the Bible, in 1 Samuel 1 and 2, is the story of a woman named Hannah. She was married to a man named Elkanah, who loved her dearly. God had closed Hannah's womb, which was a divine detour, so she could not have children. Hannah prayed year after year, asking God to bless her with a son. What made Hannah so distraught is that Elkanah had another wife named Peninnah, who had no difficulty having children. Every year, Peninnah would provoke Hannah and upset her so much, taunting her about how she could not have children that brought Hannah to tears. Elkanah told her not to worry, but Hannah was very upset.

Hannah made a vow and prayed to God in faith that if he would give her a son, she would give the child to be God's servant. "She made a special promise to God and said, "Lord All-Powerful, you can see how sad I am. Remember me. Don't forget me. If you will give me a son, I will give him to you. He will be yours his whole life, and as a Nazirite, he will not drink wine or strong drink,[a] and no one will ever cut his hair."–1Samuel 1:11. Hannah was at Shiloh in the tabernacle praying one day and the priest Eli heard her and said, "Go in peace. May the God of Israel give you what you asked for."–1 Samuel 1:17. God heard Hannah's prayer and opened her womb, and she gave birth to a son and named him Samuel. Hannah cared for Samuel until he was old enough to eat solid foods and then she took him to Shiloh to the church and gave him to God as she said she would. He became a great prophet. When Hannah prayed to God that day in the temple, she prayed to God respectfully, with faith, and an attitude of humility, and that is why God granted her prayer and then gave her five other children.

God placed Hannah on a divine detour because what he wanted was more than what Hannah was praying for. God wanted a prophet, but Hannah only wanted a son. Once Hannah said she would give the son back to God to do as he chose, then God was able to bless her mightily with five more children. Faith is what will move mountains.

As you can see, God rewards those who live by faith.

"So, then faith cometh by hearing and hearing by the word of God." –Romans 10:17.

"But without faith it is impossible to please him: for he that cometh to God must believe that he is and that he is a rewarder of them that diligently seek him." –Hebrews 11:6.

"And Jesus answering saith unto them, Have faith in God. For verily I say unto you, that whosoever shall say unto this mountain, be thou removed, and be thou cast into the sea; and shall not doubt in his heart but shall believe that those things which he saith shall come to pass; he shall have whatsoever he saith. Therefore, I say unto you, what things soever ye desire, when ye pray, believe that ye receive them, and ye shall have them." –Mark 11:22-24.

"Now faith is the substance of things hoped for, the evidence of things not seen." –Hebrews 11:1.

"For by grace are ye saved through faith; and that not of yourselves: it is the gift of God: Not of works, lest any man should boast." –Ephesians 2:8-9.

"For we walk by faith, not by sight." –2 Corinthians 5:7.

Since we are made in the image of God, we are to live our daily lives living in faith, not relying on our feelings. Sometimes the rain that falls on us is because God has bigger and better things in mind for us and he must use the rain to guide us into our destiny.

Running Hot And Cold

Sometimes in life, you will run hot and cold. If you have a fever or chills, you will feel hot and cold. When you take a shower, you normally combine the hot water faucet and the cold, so it is a mixed temperature, so you don't scald your body with too much hot water, and you don't freeze your body with too much chilly water. If you're old-fashioned and wash your own dishes or if it's just yourself and maybe someone else in the household instead of running the dishwasher, you wash the dishes yourself and use the same format as the above example and mix the water temperatures. If you go into a sauna which is meant to make you sweat and remove toxins from your body while you are in there you are hot but once you come out, you need to wrap your body with a bathrobe or else you will immediately feel cold. These are all examples of running hot and cold. However, you should not be running hot and cold in your spiritual life. When Jesus sacrificed himself on the cross for you, he did not have second thoughts and ran hot and cold.

"Ye shall do my judgments, and keep mine ordinances, to walk therein: I am the Lord your God." –Leviticus 18:4

"And when he putteth forth his own sheep, he goeth before them, and the sheep follow him: for they know his voice." –John 10:4

"Then spake Jesus again unto them, saying, I am the light of the world: he that followeth me shall not walk in darkness, but shall have the light of life." –John 8:12

"For Jerusalem is ruined, and Judah is fallen: because their tongue and their doings are against the Lord, to provoke the eyes of his glory." –Isaiah 3:8

"For the children of Israel walked forty years in the wilderness, till all the people that were men of war, which came out of Egypt, were consumed, because they obeyed not the voice of the Lord: unto whom the Lord sware that he would not shew them the land, which the Lord sware unto their fathers that he would give us, a land that floweth with milk and honey."–Joshua 5:6

"But it shall come to pass, if thou wilt not hearken unto the voice of the Lord thy God, to observe to do all his commandments and his statutes which I command thee this day; that all these curses shall come upon thee, and overtake thee:" -Deuteronomy 28:15

When life is great, you are running hot. You are quick to read your bible, follow your bible, go to church, follow the golden rule, give your tithes to the church, help your neighbor, be kind to a co-worker, volunteer your time at organizations, give to charities, etc.

When life is testing your faith, then you are running cold. You have no intention of reading your bible because God is not answering your prayers. You don't even know where the bible is. Going to church is the last thing on your mind. You don't want to follow the golden rule because why should you be nice to others when you are in pain with your personal issues? I need every penny I can get my hands on, so why should I tithe? There are many other people in the church who are tithing, so the church doesn't need my money. I can save my tithe money, so I can buy all my Starbucks lattes for the week which I need to keep me awake to go to this treacherous job where nobody cares and are the most ungrateful bunch of people I have ever encountered. My neighbor can ask someone else to borrow their lawnmower because I'm not the only person on the block. I work 60 or more hours per week, so I don't have time to be kind to a co-worker or volunteer my time at different organizations. I am not donating or giving to any charities because I am a charity case myself. WOW, that was a mouthful! Let me take a breath. God provided us all with a beautiful thing called memory and remembrance. Let's reflect a moment, shall we?

1-Even though your credit score is not 800, God got you approved for that brand-new car when your old car, the clunker that it is, was on its last leg.

2-There have been three rounds of layoffs at your job within the last year, but you are still employed, so you can continue to pay for that new car.

3-You don't have healthcare, but God continues to keep you healthy and strong where you can move around on your own and you still have use of your five senses.

4-Sometimes you didn't have enough money to pay your cell phone bill or buy groceries for the week, but you have that trusty old water bottle in your place where you could take out all the coins and change and go to the supermarket and put them in the coin star machine and then go to the customer service desk and get bills and handle what you need to.

5- What about the times when you wrote a check to pay a bill for a disconnect and you are hoping the check doesn't clear the bank before your pay is direct deposited? You get lucky and it works for your good.

There are countless other examples that I can use, but I know you all get my drift. Remember what the Bible says, "Let your conversation be without covetousness; and be content with such things as ye have: for he hath said, I will never leave thee, nor forsake thee." -Hebrews 13:5. "For God so loved the world, that he gave his only begotten Son, that whosoever believeth in him should not perish, but have everlasting life."–John 3:16. "If my people, which are called by my name, shall humble themselves, and pray, and seek my face, and turn from their wicked ways; then will I hear from heaven, and will forgive their sin, and will heal their land."–2 Chronicles 7:14. "Trust in the Lord with all thine heart, and lean not unto thine own understanding. In all thy ways acknowledge him, and he shall direct thy paths."–Proverbs 3:5-6.

Don't become arrogant, angry, flighty, disgruntled when you, as a just person, have some rain fall on you, reflect on all the grace God has given you. God has made some powerful promises to us, and if we would just be obedient and heed his words, we will be abundantly blessed. Stop Running Hot and Cold, God doesn't.

Choices

Every day that God provides us with the breath of life, we are presented with choices. What am I going to eat for breakfast, lunch, and dinner? Am I going to do intermittent fasting today? When I go to the gym, what type of workouts am I going to engage in today? Am I going to work on that proposal for work today or am I going to clear up some backed-up issues? I have a nail appointment after work what color should I have my nails painted and do I want a design? Should I carry an umbrella today since the weather report says there may be rain? The list is endless of all the choices that can be presented to us each day. However, are we being prudent and using wisdom when we make these choices?

"My son, if thou wilt receive my words, and hide my commandments with thee; So that thou incline thine ear unto wisdom, and apply thine heart to understanding; Yea, if thou criest after knowledge, and liftest up thy voice for understanding. –Proverbs 2:1-3. When we are young, we don't always use prudence when we are making choices but when we get older, we are supposed to become wiser however unfortunately a lot of us don't and that is the reality. Recently, a man I know wanted to give his girlfriend a fabulous time celebrating her birthday. He made a reservation at a charming hotel and intended to show her an exciting time. He thought he could just have a wonderful time for the few days and then do a charge-back on his credit card regarding the hotel and get his money back. The credit card company deposited the funds back onto his card after he issued the charge-back. What he didn't expect is that an investigation would be done and after they completed it, when he least expected it, they withdrew all his funds regarding the hotel expense from his credit card, and that left him overdrawn and despondent.

We all make mistakes, but when they are repeated, then they become a habit. Some habits are good, and others are not so good. Making choices to trust God no matter what makes Satan get up and then he sits up and takes notice. Are you aware that you make 2,500 choices daily? Every time you make a wise choice, it makes the devil angry. Keeping faith and belief in God is another great choice. When heaven is silent, and you are crying out for a manifestation, keep making the right choices. Even if you spiral downward, remember once you get all the way to the bottom, if that happens, there is nowhere else to go but up.

Be careful regarding the choices you make daily because as we grow older, we should give up foolishness and have the maturity of mind.

When Things Don't Make Sense

We all have seasons we go through as we live this journey that is called life. We all are most joyful when we are in a harvest season. That means everything is going our way and coming up like roses. There are no struggles or challenges that come up and whatever our hands touch, prospers.

However, we all realize that there is also a winter season, and that does not bring pleasant things. Winter seasons are harsh and grueling. Everything we try to do backfires and blows up in our face. Every time you look around, all you seem to be doing is putting out fires. For every step you take forward, you are being pulled back five. Why is this happening? This is when things don't make sense.

You worked very hard for that promotion, yet someone who doesn't have anywhere near the qualifications you do passed you over. Your offering bid for that dream home you want was declined and someone who didn't offer as much was approved. You have changed the way you eat, and you are eating healthier and exercising, yet when you take your A1C test, your blood sugar levels are still through the roof. You are in the choir in your church; you are one of the teachers for the Sunday's school classes in church; you are also an usher, but when it is time to be selected as a board member in the church, they passed you over. For years, you have been praying for God to open your uterus so you can have a baby. Finally, the pregnancy test is positive, and you carry your baby almost full term only to have a miscarriage. Your spouse and you are godly people and attend church regularly, but while at work, you get a phone call from the police that says your spouse has just committed suicide. What is happening? My spouse never showed signs of having mental health issues. Where is God?

When things don't make sense, don't panic. God is still in control. To the natural man, it does not appear that way. God, however, is supernatural. He knows things we don't. When God designed you, he knew every disappointment, every hurt you would encounter. Sometimes we go through arduous winter seasons because God is trying to improve us. There are things inside of us he needs to remove and grow us up and those things don't happen when we are in a harvest season, and everything is going great. You're wondering why that dream of yours is taking so long. Well, maybe what you are dreaming for is much smaller than what God has in mind for you and so it's taking longer. The longer what you desire takes to manifest that is because it is going to be so much greater than what you expected. If you are dealing with some very tragic and dramatic events in your life, that is because God knows you will have some rougher waters ahead of you in your future and so he needs to prepare you now. You are stronger than you think. Remember, you can do all things through Christ that strengthens you.

When things don't make sense, don't abandon all the good things you have been doing. Keep being good to people, keep tithing in church, keep going to church, continue to be a person of integrity, and above all continue to thank God and have gratitude because when God provides you with your breakthrough it will be so dynamic and monumental you will say look at what the Lord has done.

Chapter 15

You Are Closer Than You Think

Many people give up on their dreams at the wrong time. When people have been working at something for so long and it just isn't turning into what they hoped it would, they just give up. Well, what does giving up and throwing in the towel solve? If it is a dream God has placed that in your heart, I can guarantee you that you may decide to give up on it, but God never will. When you decide to give up, then you have decided to just be miserable.

When you have a fixation on something, that is something that God has designed for you. Whether that is to be an engineer, actor, writer, pastor, sports athlete, baker, singer, painter, clothes designer, etc. If every time you try to divert your thoughts to something else, but this one thing keeps coming back, that is the imagination God has placed in you. What is imagination according to Albert Einstein? "Imagination is everything. It is the preview of life's coming attractions." Well, we all know what previews are, especially when it comes to the movies. When you go to the movies and the theatre runs about 20 minutes of previews for upcoming new release movies according to what you see, that determines whether you want to go see the movies when it is released.

I've heard it said that many people give up when they are at the 1-yard line. Since no of us have a crystal ball to see into the future, that is possible. However, that is where faith and trust in God must kick in at an even higher gear. When you have been waiting for a long time for something, that means that what you want is going to be bigger and better than what you hoped for.

Letitia Wright an actress who was an award winner in 2018 for the Teen Choice Award in the category for Choice Sci-Fi Movie Actress in the motion picture Black Panther, in 2019 for the Screen Actors Guild Awards for the category of Outstanding Performance by a Cast in the Motion Picture Black Panther, also in 2019 for the British Academy Film Awards for the category of Rising Star Award for the motion picture Black Panther, and in 2022 for NAACP Image Awards for Outstanding Character Voice-Over Performance for the motion picture Sing 2 didn't know how close she was to mega success.

Ms. Wright, who has amassed all these accolades who is just 28 years of age, was born in Georgetown, Guyana. Seven years later, her family moved to London, England. When Ms. Wright was receiving the award for Rising Star at the BAFA she stated the following, "A few years ago, I saw myself in a deep state of depression and I literally wanted to quit acting. The only thing that pulled me out of it was God, my belief, my faith, and my family, and an email from BAFTA asking me to become part of the BAFTA Breakthrough Brits, I was like: 'Let me try again.'" https://www.usatoday.com/story/life/people/2019/02/12/black-panther-letitia-wright-almost-quit-acting-depression-struggle/2845821002/https://en.wikipedia.org/wiki/Letitia_Wright

This is the reason you never give up on your dreams, because you never know what bountiful blessings God has in store for you and you never know that you are closer than you think.

Look Forward–Move Forward–Press Forward

"Study the past if you would define the future." - Confucius

"We keep moving forward, opening new doors and doing new things, because we're curious, and curiosity keeps leading us down new paths."–Walt Disney

"If you can't fly then run, if you can't run then walk, if you can't walk then crawl, but whatever you do you have to keep moving forward." Martin Luther King Jr

"If we fail to adapt, we fail to move forward." John Wooden

"Let us move forward with strong and active faith." Franklin D. Roosevelt

"A man who is pressing forward to accomplish worthy goals can soon put despondency under his feet."–Ezra Taft Benson

We were made in the image of God, and he pressed forward for six days to create the earth. Life happens and things go haywire sometimes, but we must keep going forward. God gives us a new set of grace every 24 hours and gives us an anointing to go through.

If you scheduled an Amtrak excursion on the "Empire Builder" from Spokane WA which travels through mountains and long tunnels you wouldn't tell the train conductor to stop the train before the tunnel because you are afraid of going through and what you may run into on the other side. Your eyes and heart would be lit up with excitement for what would come next.

This is the same way we must handle life daily. We must jump in with both feet and know that God will carry us safely through to the other side. We cannot cringe in fear or stop living our lives that isn't the life that Jesus died for us to have. "The thief cometh not, but for to steal, and to kill, and to destroy: I am come that they might have life and that they might have it more abundantly."–John 10:10.

We all have days when the pain is so real that we feel like we cannot breathe. We don't want to get out of bed. It feels like we cannot talk to anyone and so we shut out the world. Whether it be the loss of a loved one, a divorce, the loss of a job, a friend walked out on you, someone double-crosses you, you don't know where your next dollar is coming from to eat. Remember, God is with you always. Remember what God said, "Fear thou not; for I am with thee: be not dismayed; for I am thy God: I will strengthen thee; yea, I will help thee; yea, I will uphold thee with the right hand of my righteousness."–Isaiah 41:10

Even though rain falls on the just, we realize that we cannot just bury our heads in the sand and stop moving forward. Sometimes God presents us with Divine Detours in life, which is what will bring us into the magnificent life he has designed for us if we keep looking forward, moving forward, & pressing forward trusting him.

One such story is about a woman named Liz Murray. She was raised by parents who lived a drug addicted life. At the young age of 15, Liz was homeless. Her mother had passed away from HIV and her father had moved into a homeless shelter. Liz, however, continued to move forward and went to a local high school, graduated and continued to press forward and received a scholarship to Harvard. Liz now is an American memoirist and inspirational speaker. Her life story was told in Lifetime's television film Homeless to Harvard, The Liz Murray Story. Liz also wrote a memoir titled Breaking Night: A Memoir of Forgiveness, Survival, and My Journey from Homeless to Harvard, that was published in 2010 and became a New York Times Bestseller. Liz had this to say about her challenges in life, "Instead, what I was beginning to understand was that however things unfolded from here on, whatever the next chapter was, my life could never be the sum of one circumstance. It would be determined, as it had always been, by my willingness to put one foot in front of the other, moving forward, come what may." life/may." https://www.morefamousquotes.com/topics/quotes-about-moving-to-the-next-chapter-in-life/

Murray has received numerous accolades and awards, including the White House Project's Role Model Award, Oprah Winfrey's first-ever Chutzpah Award in 2004 and Alex Award in 2011. Winfrey's Chutzpah Award is given to women, who show boldness and courage, go against the odds and have achieved greatness. In 2008, she received Appalachian Women's Fund's Women of Vision Award. On May 19, 2013, she was awarded an honorary doctorate of public service and gave the commencement address at Merrimack College in North Andover, Massachusetts. https://en.wikipedia.org/wiki/Liz_Murray

One Step At A Time

Why is it important for all of us to take one step at a time? Our creator, God, did so. If we are to emulate him, then we should do the same thing.

Let me provide you with some things that go one step at a time:

1–A baby. Many babies take their first steps between the age of 9 months and 12 months. Babies, just like all of us, must take one step at a time. They must learn to walk before they can run.

2- A ladder. When we open a ladder to use it, we go up one step at a time. For all of you WWE fans, which is almost everybody, you know about the ladder matches. They are excited to see when a wrestler has knocked all the other ones down and climbs the ladder to reach the championship belt and be declared the winner. For those of you who don't follow wrestling, you also know you can only climb one step at a time.

3- A recipe. When we decide to prepare some food that we have never fixed before, we look up the dish and find a recipe. We purchase all the ingredients that we will need and follow the instructions carefully, one step at a time. For example, for the holidays you want to make Gingerbread Cookies. That's great, but you need to follow the recipe. The most important thing you must do is chill the dough for at least 3 hours. If you just wrap it and then roll it out after a while and try to start making the shapes without chilling it, you will have a disaster. You want your cookie dough firm, so the cookies hold their shape. You won't have that unless you have chilled cookie dough.

4- A Christmas Tree. If you decorate a Christmas tree for the holidays, you know it is a step-by-step process. First, you purchase the tree. Then spread out the branches. Then you must place it in a tree stand. You also need a tree skirt. Then you add the festive decorations you have purchased. One by one, you add the lights, tinsel, bulbs, ornaments, ribbons, etc.

These are all examples of taking things one step at a time. Don't rush life because it goes quickly on its own. If God showed the utmost patience by creating the world one step at a time, why can't we?

American gymnast Simone Biles is no stranger to taking one step at a time. At just 25 years of age, she has won seven Olympic Medals and 25 World Championship medals. In 2020, ahead of the Olympics, she stated, "Right now, my mindset is to kind of take everything one day at a time, one step at a time because you never know what will happen and you can't take any training for granted. Kind of live in the moment." This year, July 7, 2022, they presented Simone with Presidential Medal of Freedom. It is the nation's highest honor given to civilians. President Joe Biden gave that to her in a ceremony at the White House. She is the youngest person to ever receive this award. https://en.wikipedia.org/wiki/Simone_Biles.

Take the first step in faith. You don't have to see the whole staircase, just take the first step."–Martin Luther King Jr.

Chess And Life

To achieve our goal in life, we must take the initiative. We must also do the same when playing chess. In life and in chess, we must decide what to keep and what to discard and ensure the proper timing of our decisions. To achieve our greatest goal in life, as well as in chess, we must make certain sacrifices.

Humanity seeks answers about life, death, and the existence of God as we play chess against the devil. Both life and chess involve strategic thinking, tactical thrust, and positional play. Like the three stages of life; childhood, youth, and adulthood- Chess has three stages; opening, middle game, and end game. In the game of chess, to begin with, there are rules, and the end is to capture the castle of the other which humans have attempted from the beginning of time.

It is widely accepted by most historians that the game of chess originated in India. Like most competitive situations, chess offers a litany of positive learning experiences. Cognitive abilities, logic, strategy, etc. However, there are some elements of chess so rich in value that they should not be overlooked. The similarities to life are astounding.

Accountability - Nowhere in sports nor nearly any competitive environment does there exist a situation where 100% control of the outcome is completely within your hands. In chess, the entire competition is internal. There aren't any elements that can influence this outcome outside the realm of your own mind.

Creativity - Many chess battles are defined by electrifying moves that abruptly change the dynamics of the game. Often, the most unexpected moves are the most potent. Few competitive environments promote imagination as a resource for handling seemingly inevitable defeat.

Falling Short - Learning from your past mistakes is one of your greatest assets. Assessing what doesn't work is one of the core elements of improvement. Yet in few other places, do you get to experience the process of learning from failure as you do in chess?

Individuality - When playing the game of chess, you are forced to rely entirely on your own thought process. Competitions abound, but few that take place entirely within your mind. When your mind is thinking empowering thoughts, and this leads to victory, you develop confidence in your ability to solve problems using your own mind rather than external sources.

Patience—There goes that word again—Patience. For those of us that have a Type A personality where we want things completed days ago, this is not good news. However, this is precisely what is required to help you win chess games. In chess, particularly at the beginner levels, when the propensity for blunders is high, avoiding your own mistakes can win you a lot of games. The difference in chess is that errors are reduced by developing patience rather than technique.

Wisdom—As you continue to persevere and never give up, you will gain wisdom in the game.

When you see a good move, look for a better one. –Emanuel Lasker

The game of chess is the most fascinating and intellectual pastime which the wisdom of antiquity has bequeathed to us. –Howard Staunton

We are formed by little scraps of wisdom. –Umberto Eco

Every day we all are to live a life of accountability like Jesus did when he was here on earth. God blessed us all with unique gifts and we are to work with those gifts to produce our creativity. We are not to dwell on failure or falling short because God is continuously keeping us on the Potter's Wheel molding and refining us daily. We are to be proud of our individuality because God created each one of us differently, so we would all bring something of greatness to this world. Patience is something that all of us will have to gain. God will continue to work with us and test us until we have it. Think about how patient Noah had to be when he was building the ark and once the rains came and ceased after forty days until the waters abated and he and his family could come out of the ark. If nothing else, can you imagine the patience he, his wife, and children had to have for the smell of the ark with all the waste from all the animals? Remember, there was no Febreze in those days! If that example does not resonate with you think about Joseph and the patience, he had to have from the time he had a dream at 17 years of age that he would be the ruler of Egypt, and it didn't manifest until 13 years later. Finally, wisdom, we are all to crave, pray, and desire wisdom. In the Bible, there is an entire book dedicated to just wisdom with 31 chapters. If it wasn't important, it wouldn't be there.

So, when you are feeling overwhelmed and angry that life is dumping loads of rain on you like when there is a hurricane just pull out your chess board and grab a friend or family member and have a friendly game and remember nothing in life is permanent things are temporary and this too shall pass.

Trust God Always

Where does your trust lie? Is it in humanity or God? Humanity comprises feelings and emotions which can be very fickle sometimes. The definition of fickle is as follows: marked by a lack of steadfastness, constancy, or stability given to erratic changeableness. –www. https://www.merriam-webster.com/dictionary/f ickle. So now that you know the definition, you know that at some time in your life; you have been fickle as well. God, however, is consistent and never changes or is fickle. "For I am the Lord, I change not". –Malachi 3:6. Since God never changes, we should have our entire trust in him always.

Why is it so easy for us to trust other things so easily? For example, at amusement parks, there is always a big draw for rollercoasters. The lines to get on the ride are incredible. Why is it, though, we climb into the roller coaster giddy, sweaty, pumped with adrenaline, and trust that the ride will be exceptional? We never have wavering trust that our feet will never land safely on solid ground within 3 1/2 to 4 minutes after the inception of the ride. So, if we are so confident and stable and grounded in our trust in a man-made steel object, why is our trust so flimsy in our creator?

The most amazing trust story comes in the book of Genesis regarding Abraham. Sarah and Abraham waited 25 years to have a child. God promised Abraham a son, but he was waiting for 25 years. When Isaac was born, Abraham was 100 years old, and his wife Sarah was 90 years old. God tempted Abraham one day to see where his trust lied by telling him to kill Isaac. Abraham took Isaac to a mountain that God told him to and sacrifice Isaac there. Abraham tied Isaac down and, just as he drew his knife to kill him, an angel of the Lord advised Abraham to stop. The angel of the lord said to Abraham, because you have not withheld your one and only son and was ready to kill him God says he will bless you and make of you a great nation.

Abraham's trust did not lie in people it was with God. Even though he had to wait 25 years for Isaac, he still obeyed God and was willing to sacrifice Isaac. Some of us don't want to even wait 25 minutes for something, let alone destroy the thing we have waited so long for. The Bible says, "Blessed is that man that maketh the Lord his trust, and respecteth not the proud, nor such as turn aside to lies." -Psalm 40:4.

American gospel and contemporary Christian recording artist Mandisa knows trusting God is what will bring you back from the edge of life. Mandisa was a contestant on American Idol back in 2006 until she was eliminated on April 5, 2006. Mandisa has had to overcome many issues in her life. One of them overeating an addiction to food. She reached success by losing 100 lbs. and reaching her weight goal. However, she had a relapse back in 2013 when she lost a good friend to breast cancer. Mandisa went into a downward spiral and gained back much of the weight she had lost along with having severe bouts of depression and thoughts of suicide. With all this happening, she went into seclusion and was not seen in public again until 2017. She has now since emerged and has written a book titled "Out of the Dark: My Journey Through the Shadows to Find God's Joy." With the release of her book Mandisa shares how God helped her come out of those dark places and how she hopes her story will help others to trust God.

Unless you are an infant and if you are, then you could not possibly be reading this book you too have had some experience with God. Everyone encounters highs and lows in their lives, but there is always a moment when you thought that was it and God came through. Remember, even when you are a just person and having seasons of rain falling on you just think when you are driving if there is a bridge above you there is a shelter called an overpass that you can pull over and stay there until the rain lightens up. God is your overpass in life. Just trust him.

Chapter 16

Gratitude

The key to continual elevation in life is gratitude. – Isaac Oyedepo

"In everything give thanks: for this is the will of God in Christ Jesus concerning you". - 1 Thessalonians 5:18.

The definition of gratitude is the state of being grateful: thankfulness. - http: //www.merriam-webster.com

"Do not spoil what you have by desiring what you have not; remember that what you now have was once among the things you only hoped for." - Epicurus. He was an ancient Greek philosopher as well as the founder of the school of philosophy called Epicureanism.

"The single greatest thing you can do to change your life today would be to start being grateful for what you have right now. And the more grateful you are, the more you get." -Oprah.

Most things in life come in upgrades: Used car - Brand new car; Apartment - House; Boyfriend - Husband; Laundromat - Twin set Washer & Dryer. For those of you that are old school - Beepers & Pagers - Cell Phone. There is an old saying " a dollar and a dream" but nowadays, as most of you are aware, most scratch-off lotto tickets are two dollars and above. There are countless individuals who have won the lottery and lost it all. All of us have the capability to dream but, we should not forget to have gratitude for what we already have.

Gratitude is the essential oil that its perfume aroma reaches the nostrils of GOD and rains down showers of blessings! Gratitude is not just done verbally; it is also done physically.

You have an old car that you feel is more trouble than it's worth, but it beats walking. While you're dreaming about the new car, you want to keep this old one clean and do the maintenance. This is an example of gratitude for what you have.

You live in the projects, and there is no laundry facility. You must take your dirty clothes in a bag in a shopping cart and walk several blocks to the coin-operated laundromat. Be grateful that you have the ability and movement in your arms and legs to walk and push the shopping cart until you upgrade to an apartment that has a laundry facility in the apartment complex. This is an example of gratitude for what you have.

You've been married for several years, and the fire is not as high in flames like the Bellagio Fountain in Las Vegas. All you two do is fight and argue all the time. Be grateful that at least you have someone to fight and argue with because there are loads of single people that would love to trade places with you and cancel their online romantic connection site. This is an example of gratitude for what you have:

REMEMBER THE MAGIC WORDS AND SAY THEM DAILY AT LEAST THREE TIMES LIKE THE TRINITY. THANK YOU, THANK YOU, THANK YOU.

"Cultivate the habit of being grateful for every good thing that comes to you, and to give thanks continuously. And because all things have contributed to your advancement, you should include all things in your gratitude." - ———— Ralph Waldo Emerson

"Let gratitude be the pillow upon which you kneel to say your nightly prayer. And let faith be the bridge you build to overcome evil and welcome good." - ——— Maya Angelou, Celebrations: Rituals of Peace and Prayer

"To be grateful is to recognize the Love of God in everything He has given us - and He has given us everything. Every breath we draw is a gift of His love, every moment of existence is a grace, for it brings with it immense graces from Him. Gratitude, therefore, takes nothing for granted, is never unresponsive, is constantly awakening to new wonder and to praise of the goodness of God. For, the grateful person knows that God is good, not by hearsay but by experience. And that is what makes all the difference." - Thomas Merton

"God gave you a gift of 86,400 seconds today. Have you used one to say thank you," - William Arthur Ward

"Gratitude is riches. Complaint is poverty." –Doris Day

Unsure of how to verbalize gratitude, try this:

Dear GOD, I am grateful for life because it helps me to be thankful and appreciate the sun, the moon, water, food, flowers, rainbows, storms, my health, my job, the money I have, and the relationships I have. If you did not breathe the breath of life in me daily, I could not indulge in any of these things. I just want to show my gratitude for what I have now while you are preparing an even brighter future for me. Amen. Daily in the morning before you start your day, make a list of at least 10 things to be grateful for. Not only will this keep you in a state of being grateful, but it will also set the course for your day when all the little annoyance that come up and try to get you into thinking negatively you will stray away from.

GRATITUDE...INDULGE IN IT....AND PASS IT ALONG TO OTHERS!!!!!!!!!!!!!!!!!!!!!!!!!!!!!!!!

You Are Blessed

The next day is not promised to any of us. Therefore, we must live in the present, the here and now. However, not every day is smooth sailing. We sometimes get thrown a curveball like in baseball that throws us off-kilter. No matter what, you must constantly remember you are blessed. There is always someone who is dealing with an even bigger battle than you are. "I cried because I had no shoes until I met a man who had no feet."–Helen Keller.

Examples of how you are blessed

Your car is in poor condition and runs badly. While driving, you pass several bus stops that are crowded with people who don't have a car.

You are overworked and underpaid. You go out to lunch and see there are several people in the lobby who are applying for a job with the firm where you work. They don't have a job and you have a job.

You dream of owning a home because the apartment complex where you live is poorly maintained with dim lighting and sometimes it is hard to find a parking space. While you are driving home, you see several homeless people in the street who have nowhere to sleep, asking for money and pulling a shopping cart.

You have a cold, and it's making you miserable. You are constantly coughing and blowing your nose. You take some cough medicine and put some tissues in your bag and head over to the hospital to visit your friend who has pneumonia.

You sign up to take a tour, however; it is not what you thought it would be. There is too much walking, and your legs are hurting, and your feet are sore. You meet someone else on the tour who is confined to a wheelchair and cannot see everything they want because of the terrain where they cannot get to certain places with the wheelchair.

You go to the movies with your friends, and you are disappointed because the cinematography is not as breathtaking as you expected. Then you see someone at the movies who is vision impaired.

Your spouse aggravates you to no end and sometimes you wish they weren't around. You get a phone call from your best friend, who is hysterically crying because their spouse just passed away suddenly.

Every day you wake up, you are blessed. That means God still has a purpose for your life. You are blessed when you have clean water to drink; you have a washer and dryer where you live; you have a vehicle to drive; you have all your five senses working; you have your health; you have food to eat, your parents are still alive and in good health, living on their own and not in a facility. Your children have a heart for God, and they are serving him in some capacity in the church.

As you can see, there are so many ways in which God blesses us daily, from the smallest to the greatest. Having your eyesight to seeing a rainbow and a butterfly is just as great as taking a month-long tour of Europe. Thank God daily for all his blessing and remember YOU ARE BLESSED!

Treasure Every Moment

Life is a gift and at any moment, it can become extinct. Therefore, it is important to treasure every moment. This is the reason we need to listen and reflect on one of country music singer Tim McGraw's popular songs "Live Like You Were Dying."

It is possible that you have not encountered this situation personally, but I am sure you have heard of someone who had a huge argument with someone, and things got blown out of proportion and then they either received a phone call or a visit and was advised that person passed away. That becomes a dreadful moment in the person's life that is still alive because they never have time to apologize or correct the situation. Life is fleeting and just like the Bible says, "Whereas ye know not what shall be on the morrow. For what is your life? It is even a vapour, that appeareth for a little time, and then vanisheth away."–James 4:14

If you are fortunate to have both of your parents or even one still alive, treasure that. If you have been blessed to have a spouse, realize how blessed you are since there are so many single people out there looking for true love and hoping to find their soul mate. The Bible says, "Two are better than one, because they have a good reward for their labour. For if they fall, the one will lift up his fellow: but woe to him that is alone when he falleth; for he hath not another to help him up. Again, if two lie together, then they have heat: but how can one be warm alone?" -Ecclesiastes 4:9-11. Treasure your spouse. If you are a parent and have been blessed with children treasure them because they are a gift from God. There are countless people who wanted to have a child of their own and it was not in the cards and so they have adopted or just remained without children. Remember, the Bible says, "Lo, children are an heritage of the Lord: and the fruit of the womb is his reward."–Psalm 127:3.

Treasure moments with your family members even if you have one or some in your family that is like Walter (Jeff Dunham's Puppet). You know exactly what I mean: hard to get along with and crotchety. Treasure the fact that you have a place of employment to go to or, even better, if you are working from home. There are so many people out of work now. It may not be what you want it to be, but it is something that is better than nothing. Our animals bring us such happiness and joy and we spend lots of money on them. They are to be treasured as well because they get the same sickness and diseases we get, and we can lose them at any time. Treasure and respect your grandparents if they are still alive because they have something more precious than ever, which is wisdom. Pray and ask God to bless you with long life like them.

Every day we hear about tragic losses people must endure and they are heartbreaking. Recently it was listed in the news about a couple whose 9-month-old daughter died of cancer. There was also an article about a newlywed couple who died in a tragic car accident after only being married for three days. Recently, an awfully close friend of mine lost her fiancé. He died in his sleep two days before Christmas. They already had their wedding date set. One can only imagine the devastation she is feeling. "Treasure every moment in our life and take the time to ensure the story we create is one that we will be proud of and look back with a huge smile."–Kanya Puspokusumo

A family member of mines always says, "Thank God for life." I have adopted that phrase and say it often because she knows what she is talking about. God has blessed her to live 95 years so far. I have also heard quite a few people say the phrase "God willing." Well, this is a phrase we should take seriously as well because the Bible says, "A man's mind plans his way as he journeys through life, But the Lord directs his steps and establishes them."–Proverbs 16:9.

Recently the Macon family of Savannah GA had to endure the loss of a daughter, sister, & brother because of a senseless crime. Brittany Nicole Macon worked at a Subway restaurant in Atlanta GA and was murdered because of a dispute between a customer and her regarding too much mayo on a sandwich the customer ordered. Another employee of the restaurant was also shot but was taken to a hospital and was in critical condition. The other employee was in the Subway restaurant with her 5-year-old son who was not injured. May God bring comfort to this family at this tragic time.

Remember, the next moment is not promised to any of us, so treasure every moment that is pleasing to God.

Bonus

Bonus - something in addition to what is expected or strictly due.

Here are some examples of types of bonuses: All references taken from https://www.merriam-webster.com.

1- money or an equivalent given in addition to an employee's usual compensation

2-a premium as of stock given by a corporation to a purchaser of its securities, to a promoter, or to an employee

3-a government payment to war veterans

4-a sum in excess of salary given to an athlete for signing with a team

We all like to get a bonus and are excited when we get what we are expecting. However, what happens when we do not get what we wanted? We then become annoyed, exasperated, and a host of other negative emotions. The mind is a BATTLEFIELD. Let us take a closer look at how we have choices and how we can look at a bonus in a negative or positive mindset.

B = Broken or Beauty for Ashes. We can choose to feel broken, shattered, crushed because we didn't get what we wanted or we can TRUST God that he will make it up to us and give us something even better and give us Beauty for Ashes and keep moving forward. "To appoint unto them that mourn in Zion, to give unto them beauty for ashes, the oil of joy for mourning, the garment of praise for the spirit of heaviness; that they might be called trees of righteousness, the planting of the Lord, that he might be glorified."–Isaiah 61:3

O = Overwhelmed or Omega. When we are in a fiery furnace like how Shadrach, Meshach, & Abednego were, we again have choices. We can become overwhelmed where all we do is stay on the phone calling friends and keep talking about all the problems and get even more stressed and overwhelmed, or we can turn to Omega for help. In the book of Revelations 22:13, "I am Alpha and Omega, the beginning and the end, the first and the last." We must have complete

FAITH in God that he will keep his promises. "For the Lord God is a sun and shield: the Lord will give grace and glory: no good thing will he withhold from them that walk uprightly."–Psalm 84:11

N = Nobody or Nirvana. What about the times when we have encountered so many terrible events in our lives that we feel God has forgotten about us and we are just a nobody? We can either wallow in that negativity or we can shake that off and remember nirvana. This is a place or state of oblivion to care, pain, or external reality. https://www.merriam-webster.com.

An example of this would be a resort which is a skier's and snowboarder's nirvana. Now, remember whatever provides you bliss, that is what you want to do to take yourself out of the doldrums. Remember, nothing that happens to you is a surprise to God, so let him handle it. Let Go and Let God!

U = Unworthy or Ubiquity. Sometimes in life when we think we have committed so much sin that we are unworthy to have anything good happen to us. We feel we cannot ask God for anything because we do not deserve it. Remember, God gives us all a fresh set of grace every 24 hours. Ubiquity - presence everywhere or in many places, especially simultaneously: OMNIPRESENCE. https://ww w.merriam-webster.com/dictionary/ubiquity. God is always everywhere. "The eyes of the Lord are in every place, beholding the evil and the good."–Proverbs 15:3. We must not persecute ourselves because sometimes we fall short. God sees everything we do, and he is aware of all the times you do the right thing as well as when you make a mistake. God is a loving father and wants to give the best to his children. "For thou, Lord, wilt bless the righteous; with favour wilt thou compass him as with a shield."–Psalm 5:12

S = Screwed or Success. There will come a time when we will all feel like we have had the air taken out of our sails and we have been screwed. However, what we must remember is just like how Joseph went from the Pit to the Palace, we will as well. Success may not come when you want it because God does not operate on our timetable. This is when we must dig our heels in and BELIEVE success is on the way. To everything there is a season and even though you may be in the summer season where you are pulling a lot of weeds and dealing with a lot of stressful issues remember that the spring season is on the way, and you will get your harvest. "Therefore, I say unto you, what things soever ye desire, when ye pray, believe that ye receive them, and ye shall have them."–Mark 11:24. Trust God, Have Faith and Believe for your BONUS.

Chapter 17

What Is Your Level Of Expectancy

What do you look forward to in life? Are you expecting the favor of God to shine down on your life? If not, why? "For the Lord God is a sun and shield: the Lord will give grace and glory: no good thing will he withhold from them that walk uprightly." – Psalm 84:11.

What are you expecting for your life? Do you pray bold prayers, or do you ask for as little as possible? What you expect in life is what you will receive in life. Yes, we all have challenges in life, but you should be expecting to overcome every challenge and curve ball life throws your way. If you are not expecting things to improve then nothing will. God meets his children at their expectancy level. The Bible says, "Now faith is the substance of things hoped for, the evidence of things not seen." – Hebrews 11:1. What are you hoping for in life? Begin to expect that every trial that comes your way in life you will overcome it.

In the Bible there is a very short excerpt about a man named Jabez. Now the first thing that is worth mentioning is that the name Jabez means pain. The Bible does not tell us much about this man but what we do know is that he was suffering. From the little that was written about him we see that he was a man with an extremely difficult life and had no hope for the future. We are also told that his mother conceived him in pain and that he was more honorable than other men. Jabez struggled to find any meaning and significance in life.

This revelation shows us that Jabez was a man that many of us can identify with in our present-day life. It appears that Jabez was a man who desired to be accepted by others and a man who wanted a relationship with God. This is what is listed in the Bible about Jabez, "And Jabez was more honourable than his brethren: and his mother called his name Jabez, saying, Because I bare him with sorrow. And Jabez called on the God of Israel, saying, oh that thou wouldest bless me indeed, and enlarge my coast, and that thine hand might be with me, and that thou wouldest keep me from evil, that it may not grieve me! And God granted him that which he requested." - 1 Chronicles 4:9-10.

Dear God, if we would all be so bold and pray to God in that fashion. This is what God desires of us. If he didn't then we would see that he never would have answered Jabez prayer. If Jabez can pray such a bold and powerful prayer, then why can't you? Jabez had nothing to lose so he put it all out there to God and expected God to not only hear his prayer but to also answer his prayer and grant him favor. Daily we should all be expecting God's favor in our lives. We cannot go through this journey of life without God so we might as well buckle down now and do our part. God created us to have fellowship with him daily and to include him in every aspect of our lives. What you think and what you do are no surprise to God because he knows everything and remember he lives within us all.

God is Alpha and Omega there is no struggle or challenge in your life that God cannot change. God is a turnaround God and when you least expect it is when he shows up and makes all things beautiful. When the rains come in life remember what the Bible says, "For his anger endureth but a moment; in his favour is life: weeping may endure for a night, but joy cometh in the morning." – Psalms 30:5.

Your Words Have Power

I realize that what I am about to say is not going to sit favorably with most of you, but you know the old saying, "tell the truth and shame the devil." Some of the rain that has fallen in your life is due to your poor mouth. What do I mean?

The words you spoke have set you on the downward spiral you are dealing with now. If you want to change your life change the words that you speak. The Bible says, "Death and life are in the power of the tongue: and they that love it shall eat the fruit thereof." -Proverbs 18:21. Ah yes, for those of you who might have been thinking I am just throwing around words no I have the Bible to back up what I am telling you! Now not every single circumstance and challenge that comes up in your life is due to the words you spoke but some of them are.

Words and Phrases you speak:

Just my luck somebody in the office got sick so that means we will all get it now probably starting with me.

Nothing good ever happens to me. Well, I guess that is just the way my life will always be.

My health will never improve.

I will never get out of debt.

I will never be able to afford that home.

That is just a pipe dream. Good things never happen to me.

I will never be able to afford a brand-new car.

Some people are just born lucky but that is not me.

I'm sure all these phrases sound familiar to you and most likely you have said at least one or more of them several times in life. The more negativity you speak the more negativity you bring into your life. All of us have done this including me. It is never too late to break the cycle. You just must start being aware of the words you speak daily. Will you slip up sometimes yes you will but sometimes is better than all the time.

Now like I said earlier there are times when you are not the cause of your fate. This was proven in the Bible with Job. He is described this way in the Bible, "There was a man in the land of Uz, whose name was Job; and that man was perfect and upright, and one that feared God, and eschewed evil." –Job 1:1. Job was a wealthy man that was extremely favored and blessed. However, one day Satan came to God and said you have a hedge of protection around Job that is why he honors you. If you were to take away everything that he has he will curse you. God agreed just to prove Satan wrong and took away, destroyed all that Job had including his animals, business, and his children. In all this Job still praised God. However, Satan came back to God and said Job needs to be harmed as well before he will curse you. God told Satan do as you wish with him but do not take his life. Satan then destroyed Job's health and placed boils all over his body. At this point the only person left alive in Job's family was his wife and she told him to curse God and die.

I have said this to you before that since God is the director of our lives, he saves the best roles for his greatest actors and Job was one of his best. God knew that Job would pass the test of any challenges, trials, or adversities he sent his way. In the end God restored not just everything that was taken from Job, but he gave him back twice as much and Job went on to live another 140 years in bliss and happiness praising God and Satan was defeated.

Sometimes you go through things because God is showing you off to Satan and his crew and putting them on notice of how awesome you are! When you are going through one winter season after another know that God is showing you off so that Satan will know that he will never have the power he desires because you are a child of God and his greatest masterpiece that shines just like the "Mona Lisa" which is on permanent display at the Louvre in Paris.

When the rains come hold your shoulders back, sick out your chest, pray to God, praise and worship God, and smile knowing that God is ordering your steps and is in the rains with you and is going to bring you out victoriously.

Your Appointed Time

We live in an extremely fast-paced world where everything needs to come to us instantly. Banks have drive-thru lanes, so people do not have to go inside the bank and wait in line. However, sometimes you must wait in line in the drive-thru even if there are two or more lanes. Almost every restaurant has drive-thru lanes as well so we can get the food fast and in the comfort of our vehicles. Surprisingly, there are some places that do not believe in instant gratification like Italy. About eight years ago my husband and I traveled to Italy for our thirtieth wedding anniversary and were shocked and surprised to know that they do not have microwaves in

Italy. The Italians believe in fresh food that is tasty and using a microwave to quickly heat up dinner is not for them.

Therefore, we have such a difficult time waiting for our appointed time for our breakthrough. God does not work on the same thought process as we do, and this keeps us frustrated. A thousand years for God is like one day. God created all of us with a specific purpose in life we are to execute. According to what that purpose is that will determine our growth time and our refining period. God will not elevate us until we are ready to handle the tremendous future, he has in store for us, so we do not crash and burn because we were not ready. The Bible says, "And we know that all things work together for good to them that love God, to them who are the called according to his purpose." –Romans 8:28. Jesus said, "The thief cometh not, but for to steal, and to kill, and to destroy I am come that they might have life and that they might have it more abundantly." –John 10:10.

We have all heard the phrase "patience is a virtue" and it really is. For those of us that are a type A personality like me, this can be a real struggle sometimes. However, God has a sense of humor because every time he tries to promote us, he gives us a test and if we fail, he will just continue to retest us until we pass. This is what the children of Israel had to go through when they were released from Egypt and kept failing the test which is why they spent 40 years in the wilderness for a trip that should have only taken 11 days.

Don't think that your time has passed and it's too late. If you are an older person, you may believe it is too late for me. No, it is not and here are several people who did not experience success until later in life. All the following examples are taken from https://www.businessinsider.com/24-people-who-became-highly-successful-after-age-40-2015-6 This list was updated by Allana Akhtar and Marguerite Ward on Aug 10, 2022,

Samuel L. Jackson has been a Hollywood staple for years now, but he'd had only bit parts before landing an award-winning role at age 43 in Spike Lee's film "Jungle Fever" in 1991.

Sam Walton had a fairly successful retail-management career in his 20s and 30s, but his path to astronomical success began at age 44, when he founded the first

Wal-Mart in Rogers, Arkansas, in 1962. Walton passed away April 5, 1992. He was 74 years old.

Julia Child worked in advertising and media before writing her first cookbook when she was 50, launching her career as a celebrity chef in 1961. Child died August 13, 2004. She was 91 years old.

Betty White was one of the most award-winning comedic actresses in history, but she didn't become an icon until she joined the cast of "The Mary Tyler Moore Show" in 1973 at age 51. White passed away December 31, 2021. She was 99 years old.

Beloved comedian Steve Carell is known for his many blockbuster hits, including "The 40-year-old Virgin" and "The Big Short." But he didn't land his hit role as Michael Scott in "The Office" until he was 42.

Tim and Nina Zagat were both 51-year-old lawyers when they published their first collection of restaurant reviews under the Zagat name in 1979. It eventually became a mark of culinary authority.

Ray Kroc spent his career as a milkshake-device salesman before buying Mc-Donald's at age 52 in 1954. He grew it into the world's biggest fast-food franchise. Kroc passed away January 14, 1984. He was 82 years old.

Laura Ingalls Wilder spent her later years writing semi-autobiographical stories using her educated daughter, Rose, as an editor. She published the first in the "Little House" books at age 65 in 1932. They soon became children's literary classics and the basis for the TV show "Little House on the Prairie." Wilder passed away February 10, 1957. She was 90 years old.

Harland Sanders, better known as Colonel Sanders, was 62 when he franchised Kentucky Fried Chicken in 1952. He sold the franchise business for $2 million 12 years later. Sanders passed away December 16, 1980. He was 90 years old.

Harry Bernstein spent a long-life writing in obscurity but finally achieved fame at age 96 for his 2007 memoir, "The Invisible Wall: A Love Story That Broke Barriers." Bernstein passed away June 3, 2011. He was 101 years old.

Arianna Huffington founded her namesake news publication, The Huffington Post, at age 55. While she worked as a political commentator and writer for her early career, the success of her digital media publication made her a household name. HuffPost later sold to AOL for $315 million.

Stan Lee created his first hit comic, "The Fantastic Four," just shy of his 39th birthday in 1961. In the next few years, he created the legendary Marvel Universe, whose characters such as Spider-Man and the X-Men became American cultural icons. Lee passed away in late 2018 at 95-years-old.

Nobel and Pulitzer Prize-winning author Toni Morrison wrote her first novel, "The Bluest Eye," at age 40, while she was working at Random House as an editor. She won her Pulitzer Prize when she was 56, and her Nobel Prize in Literature at 62. Morrison passed away August 5, 2019. She was 88 years old.

Your Appointed Time can come at any time and any age in life. Remember what the Bible says, "Though thy beginning was small, yet thy latter end should greatly increase." – Job 8:7.

Never Give Up

Stick-to-itiveness, Perseverance, Tenacity.

Jim Carrey – Oprah Winfrey – Henry Ford – Colonel Sanders – Thomas Edison – Walt Disney – Stephen King – J. K. Rowling - Steven Spielberg – Sir Isaac Newton – Vera Wang – Sidney Poitier – Albert Einstein – Fred Astaire – Theodor Seuss Geisel – Lucille Ball – Winston Churchill – Harrison Ford – Jay Z - Andrea Bocelli.

What do all these people have in common? They Never Gave Up! There are countless others who fall into this category, but I chose these to give a mixture of persons where anybody who reads this can relate. Whether you enjoy music, entrepreneurs, movies, books, food, automobiles, etc. You can be a person into music who relates to Jay Z or you can enjoy movies and relate to Sidney Poitier or Lucille Ball, Steven Spielberg, Jim Carrey, or Harrison Ford. You might be an avid book person who can relate to Stephen King, J. K. Rowling, Dr. Seuss. You could be in love with fashion and so you relate to Vera Wang. You may crave to be on TV and want to interview people and so then you relate to Oprah Winfrey even though her talents surpass that. You may have a creative inventive mind and with that in mind, you gravitate to people like Henry Ford, Thomas Edison, Walt Disney, Sir Isaac Newton, Albert Einstein. You may aspire to be in politics and tell it like it is, so you would relate to Winston Churchill. Finally, you may just love to eat and so you relate to Colonel Sanders. God has not given up on us, you don't have the right to give up on yourself. You must keep pressing forward because you never know how close you are to your breakthrough because miracles happen every day. You are closer to your victory when you face the greatest opposition.

The following information was taken from the following sources:

https://www.wanderlustworker.com/12-famous-people-who-failed-before-succeeding/

https://www.lifehack.org/articles/productivity/15-highly-successful-people-who-failed-their-way-success.html

https://www.businessinsider.com/successful-people-who-failed-at-first-2015-7

https://www.nydailynews.com/entertainment/nydn-entertainment-sidney-poitier-years-1-3051999-photogallery.html

https://www.gov.uk/government/history/past-prime-ministers/winston-churchill

https://en.wikipedia.org/wiki/Winston_Churchill

https://en.wikipedia.org/wiki/Steven_Spielberg

https://en.wikipedia.org/wiki/Stephen_King

https://en.wikipedia.org/wiki/Fred_Astaire

https://en.wikipedia.org/wiki/Albert_Einstein

https://en.wikipedia.org/wiki/Andrea_Bocelli

Jim Carrey = was raised in a low-income family. He dropped out of school at age 15 to get a job to help support the family. He auditioned for Saturday Night Live for the 1980-81 season, he failed to land the part. In an interview with Oprah Winfrey, Carrey talks about how he used the Law of Attraction by writing himself a check for $10,000,000 million dollars for "Acting Services Rendered," later placing the check in his wallet for 7 years until he received a $10,000,000 million-dollar payment for his work in Dumb and Dumber.

Oprah Winfrey = As we have all heard Oprah say her living conditions were rough, and she was sexually abused starting at the age of 9 by family members and a family friend. She did intern work at a radio station while in college. She was fired by the producer from a local television station because she was deemed "unfit for television." However, she persevered and ultimately received her own show The Oprah Winfrey Show, which was syndicated across the country.

Henry Ford = He had several failures, but he did not let them deter him. In 1899, at the age of 36 years old, Ford formed his first company, the Detroit Automobile Company, that company went bankrupt. His second attempt was in 1901 when he formed the Henry Ford Company, which he ended up leaving with the rights to his name. That company was later renamed to the Cadillac Automobile Company. However, it was Ford's third try, with the Ford Motor Company, that success bloomed.

Colonel Sanders = he worked many jobs including fireman, tire salesman, insurance salesman, and of course, a cook. In 1952 he hit the road and began trying to sell his franchise-model chicken restaurant. He traveled across the U.S. looking for someone to sell his fried chicken, and after finally getting a business deal in Utah, Kentucky Fried Chicken was born. KFC is now one of the most recognizable franchises in the world. The company grew and expanded faster than he could have ever imagined. In 1964, at the age of 74 years old, Sanders sold the company for $2 million dollars to a group of investors.

Thomas Edison = We've all heard the name before. This famous American is attributed to failing over 10,000 times to invent a commercially viable electric light bulb, but he didn't give up. When asked by a newspaper reporter if he felt like a failure and if he should give up, after having gone through over 9,000 failed attempts, Edison simply stated "Why would I feel like a failure? And why would I ever give up? I now know over 9,000 ways an electric light bulb will not work. Success is almost in my grasp." Edison went on to hold more than 1,000 patents and invented some world-changing devices, like the phonograph, practical electrical lamp, and the movie camera.

Walt Disney = The man who has affected generations to come with his cartoon creations was once considered a failure. Disney was fired by the editor in 1919 from his job at the Kansas City Star paper because he "lacked imagination and had no clever ideas." However, the man who brought us Mickey Mouse and a slew of other characters didn't stop failing there. Several more of his businesses failed before the premiere of his movie "Snow White." He went onto become the guy who redefined American childhood.

Stephen King = Stephen King grew so frustrated over his attempt to write the novel "Carrie" that he threw away the entire early draft. King's wife Tabitha found the manuscript in the trash and took it out. "Carrie" became a hit and launched his career. Stephen King an American author of horror, supernatural fiction, suspense, science fiction, and fantasy has become a tremendous success.

J.K. Rowling = Rowling is one of the most inspirational success stories of our time. Many people simply know her as the woman who created Harry Potter. But what most people don't know is what she went through prior to reaching stardom. Rowling saw herself as a failure at this time. She was jobless, divorced, penniless, and with a dependent child. She suffered through bouts of depression, eventually signing up for government-assisted welfare. J.K. Rowling was a single mom living off welfare when she began writing the first "Harry Potter" novel. Rowling is now internationally renowned for her Harry Potter series and, in US currency, became the first billionaire author.

Steven Spielberg = Steven Spielberg was rejected by the University of Southern California School of Cinematic Arts multiple times. He went on to create the first summer blockbuster with "Jaws" in 1975 and has garnered much success since then. A figure of the New Hollywood era, he is the most commercially successful director of all time. Spielberg is the recipient of various accolades, including three Academy Awards (including two Best Director wins), a Kennedy Center honor, a Cecil B. DeMille Award, and an AFI Life Achievement Award. In 2013, Time listed him as one of the 100 most influential people. After a brief hiatus, Spielberg directed the science fiction thriller Jurassic Park, the highest-grossing film ever at the time, and the Holocaust drama Schindler's List (both 1993), described as one of the greatest films ever made. In 1998, he directed the World War II epic Saving Private Ryan. Spielberg continued in the 2000s with science fiction, including A.I. Artificial Intelligence (2001), Minority Report (2002), and

War of the Worlds (2005). He also directed the children's adventure films The Adventures of Tintin (2011), The BFG (2016), and Ready Player One (2018), and the historical dramas Amistad (1997), Munich (2005), War Horse (2011), Lincoln (2012), Bridge of Spies (2015), The Post (2017), and the musical West Side Story (2021).

Sir Isaac Newton = Sir Isaac Newton left school to run the family farm and when it became evident, he could not handle that Newton went back to school to finish his basic education and was eventually enrolled in Cambridge University. Newton went on to become one of the greatest scientists of all time, revolutionizing physics and mathematics.

Vera Wang = Vera Wang failed to make the 1968 US Olympic figure-skating team. Then she became an editor at Vogue but was passed over for the editor-in-chief position. She began designing wedding gowns at age 40 and today is one of the premier designers in the fashion industry, with a business worth over $ 650 million.

Sidney Poitier = When Sidney Poitier first auditioned for the American Negro Theatre, he flubbed his lines and spoke in a heavy Caribbean accent, which made the director angrily tell him to stop wasting his time and go get a job as a dishwasher. Poitier worked on his craft and eventually became a hugely successful Hollywood star. He won an Academy Award for Best Actor ("Lillies of the Field," 1963) and helped break down the color barrier in the American film industry. Poitier was knighted by Queen Elizabeth II in 1974. From 1997 to 2007, he served as the Bahamian Ambassador to Japan. On August 12, 2009, Poitier was awarded the Presidential Medal of Freedom, the United States' highest civilian honor, by ex-President Barack Obama. In 2016, he was awarded the BAFTA Fellowship for outstanding lifetime achievement in film.

Albert Einstein = Even with Einstein's communication and behavioral problems they were not indicative of a lack of intelligence. He went on to win the Nobel prize in physics for the discovery of the photoelectric effect, and his special theory of relativity theory corrected the deficiencies of Newtonian physics. He is known for who developed the theory of relativity, one of the two pillars of modern physics (alongside quantum mechanics). His work is also known for its influence on the philosophy of science.

Fred Astaire = In one of Fred Astaire's first screen tests, an executive wrote: "Can't sing. Can't act. Slightly balding. Can dance a little." He is widely regarded as one of the most influential dancers in the history of film and television musicals. His stage and subsequent film and television careers spanned a total of 76 years. He starred in more than 10 Broadway and West End musicals, made 31 musical films, four television specials, and numerous recordings. As a dancer, his out-standing traits were an uncanny sense of rhythm, perfectionism, and innovation. His most memorable dancing partnership was with Ginger Rogers, with whom he co-starred in a series of ten Hollywood musicals during the age of Classical Hollywood cinema,

Theodor Seuss Geisel = Theodor Seuss Geisel, better known as Dr. Seuss, had his first book rejected by 27 different publishers. Dr. Seuss became a legendary children's author known around the world for classics like "The Cat in the Hat" and "Green Eggs and Ham." His books have sold over 600 million copies and have been translated into more than 20 languages by the time of his death.

Lucille Ball = Lucille Ball appeared in so many second-tier films at the start of her career that she became known as "The Queen of B Movies." She finally achieved success with the show "I Love Lucy". In 1962, Ball became the first woman to run a major television studio, Desilu Productions, which produced several popular television series, including Mission: Impossible and Star Trek.

Winston Churchill = was a British statesman, soldier and writer who served as Prime Minister of the United Kingdom from 1940 to 1945, during the Second World War, and again from 1951 to 1955. Apart from two years between 1922 and 1924, he was a Member of Parliament MP from 1900 to 1964 and represented a total of five constituencies. Ideologically an economic liberal and imperialist, he was for most of his career a member of the Conservative Party, which he led from 1940 to 1955. He was a member of the Liberal Party from 1904 to 1924.Due to many disagreements with his political party between the years of 1929-1939 he was alienated. At the outbreak of World War II on Sep. 3, 1939, Churchill was appointed to the British Admiralty, thus ending his "exile." The next year, he was elected prime minister at the age of 62. Churchill's quote showed his perseverance. "If you're going through hell, keep going." Winston Churchill was an inspirational statesman, writer, orator and leader who led Britain to victory in the Second World War. He served as Conservative Prime Minister twice - from 1940 to 1945 (before being defeated in the 1945 general election by the Labour leader Clement Attlee) and from 1951 to 1955.

Harrison Ford = After Harrison Ford's first small movie role, an executive took him into his office and told him he'd never succeed in the movie business. Ford's career went on to span six decades and has included timeless starring roles in blockbuster films like the "Star Wars" and "Indiana Jones" series. Ford's worldwide box office grosses surpass $6 billion, making Ford the second highest-grossing U.S. domestic box-office star. He now has a net worth of over $300 million dollars.

Jay Z = In 1995 when Jay-Z tried tirelessly to strike a record deal, not a single label would sign him. It led him to establish his own record company called Roc-a-fella Records with partners Damon Dash and Kareem Biggs. Eventually, he successfully negotiated a contract with Priority, later releasing his debut album entitled, Reasonable Doubt, which would eventually go on to hit platinum. Now, the musician — who's also an investor and entrepreneur who is worth 1.3 billion dollars.

Andrea Bocelli = Andrea Bocelli OMRI OMDSM (Italian: [anˈdreːa boˈtʃɛlːi]; born 22 September 1958)[1] is an Italian tenor and multi-instrumentalist.[2][3] He was born visually impaired, with congenital glaucoma, and at the age of 12, Bocelli became completely blind, following a brain hemorrhage resulting from a football accident. After performing evenings in piano bars and competing in local singing contests, Bocelli signed his first recording contract with the Sugar Music label. He rose to fame in 1994, winning the 44th Sanremo Music Festival performing "Il mare calmo della sera".

As you can see with all these people all of them believed in never giving up. Nothing in the world can take the place of persistence and determination. If you want something bad enough nothing is ever out of reach. Live your life like failure is not an option and remember the longer your good is incoming the greater it will be when it comes. If all these people from various types of backgrounds who had rains fall on their lives never gave up why should you?

Declare No Weapon Formed Against Me Shall Prosper

"No weapon that is formed against thee shall prosper, and every tongue that shall rise against thee in judgment thou shalt condemn. This is the heritage of the servants of the Lord, and their righteousness is of me, saith the Lord." –Isaiah 54:17.

Weapons come in all shapes, sizes, and forms. Weapons can be knives, guns, tanks, hand grenades, etc. There are also other types of weapons like words, racism, bigotry, prejudice, hate and the list goes on. It's amazing that God sent his son Jesus to deliver love to the world he created but so much more has evolved since Satan was exiled from heaven. "How art thou fallen from heaven, O Lucifer, son of the morning! how art thou cut down to the ground, which didst weaken the nations!" –Isaiah 14:12.

Satan starts early in the morning to corrupt us before we even get up out of bed. He tries to put all types of bad thoughts in our heads to confuse us and cause strife and make us believe God doesn't care for us. What mother who carried a child for nine months of pregnancy or possibly less if the child was born prematurely doesn't have maternal instincts for her child. A lot of men will tell you that once the baby was born, they went directly to the back of the line. If we as human being's mothers and fathers included can care so deeply for our children, the love that our heavenly father has for us supersedes and surpasses that.

Dealing with Satan daily is like a boxing match. For those of you that are avid boxing fans, you know what I mean. For every below the belt punch that Satan throws, we must counter with an uppercut. Some of the most famous boxers like Sonny Liston, Lennox Lewis, George Foreman, and Mike Tyson had the greatest uppercut which when they unloaded their opponents fell backward in the ring and lost the fight from a count-out. We have been blessed because God taught us how to deal with weapons of warfare so that we always prosper.

"Put on the whole armour of God, that ye may be able to stand against the wiles of the devil. For we wrestle not against flesh and blood, but against principalities, against powers, against the rulers of the darkness of this world, against spiritual wickedness in high places. Wherefore take unto you the whole armour of God, that ye may be able to withstand in the evil day, and having done all, to stand. Stand therefore, having your loins girt about with truth, and having on the breastplate of righteousness; And your feet shod with the preparation of the gospel of peace; Above all, taking the shield of faith, wherewith ye shall be able to quench all the fiery darts of the wicked. And take the helmet of salvation, and the sword of the Spirit, which is the word of God: Praying always with all prayer and supplication in the Spirit and watching thereunto with all perseverance and supplication for all saints." Ephesians 6:11-18.

When the world is overwhelming you with financial problems, health issues, unemployment, car issues, a divorce, death of a family member or friend, or just all the negativity on the news daily remember God has you in the palm of his hand and nothing lasts forever, and no weapon formed against you shall prosper.

Chapter 18

Success

Everybody in life wants to have success. Whether that is success in business, a marriage, a career, an intimate relationship with God, success in raising godly children, overcoming a health issue, etc. There are a lot of things that determine you having success just the same, as there are a lot of things that determine whether you become a person of influence. Many people believe people become successful because they are lucky. They were in the right place at the right time. They were born into the right family and a host of other things. However sure a person can get lucky, but to be a success that is something that must be maintained and there are several criteria that must be met for that to happen.

S = Secure, are you a secure person? Do you feel protected and at peace all the time? If not, here's what the Bible says, "And thou shalt be secure, because there is hope, yea, thou shalt dig about thee, and thou shalt take thy rest in safety."–Job 11:18. God desires for us to feel his safety and security all the time. God has a hedge of protection around you all the time, but if you don't believe it, then your unbelief, non-faith, prevents God from working miracles in your life, which brings about success.

U = Undaunted, do you become discouraged easily? Do you feel that you have been trying for too long and nothing good has happened yet? Remember what the Bible says, "And let us not be weary in well doing: for in due season we shall reap, if we faint not."–Galatians 6:9. We have discussed this previously that if your breakthrough is taking a long time, that is because God has something big in your future. Whenever you grow tired or feel that God has forgotten about you, remember Joseph and Abraham. You must set your feet like flint or better yet, like Jacob, who wrestled with the angel of God and said, "I will not let thee go, except thou bless me." Genesis 32:26. People who have success in life don't get discouraged, give up easily, become so disappointed that they quit. To be a success, you must be undaunted by whatever struggles, challenges, trials come your way.

C = Compassion, are you a person who exudes compassion? If not, why not? Jesus did, the Bible says, "And be ye kind one to another, tenderhearted, forgiving one another, even as God for your Christ's sake hath forgiven you."–Ephesians 4:32. None of us are perfect and so that means we all make mistakes. There will never come a time in your life when someone doesn't hurt you. If it hasn't happened yet, your time is coming. You will never become a successful leader, manager, marriage partner, mother, father, employer, employee, friend or more until you realize people will hurt you at some time or another, but you must rise above that and let the water roll off your back like a duck and show them compassion. No matter how perfect you think you are, and you shouldn't because the Bible clearly says that none of us are perfect, so there will come a time when you need someone to have compassion for you for what you did or said.

C = Creativity, are you using the gifts that God gave you? The Bible says you are to use your gift, "Neglect not the gift that is in thee."–1 Timothy 4:14. God has endowed us all with a gift that we are to use. Whether that is a gift for cutting lawns, baking desserts, being a hairdresser, comedian, engineer, actor or actress, pastor, sports athlete, singer, writer, mother, teacher, etc. The list is endless, but we all have a specific talent. You are to use your gift that God gave you or he will take it from you or worst because he is a God that has allowed us to make our own choices if you let your gift lay idle you will wind up taking it to your grave. That is the reason the cemeteries are the richest places on earth because of all the people who never used their gift that God gave them and never attained success and the gift died with them.

E = Enthusiasm, do you have an excitement for life? Well, you should because for everyday that God grants you the breath of life, that is another opportunity for success. The Bible says, "And whatsoever ye do, do it heartily, as to the Lord, and not unto men."–Colossians 3:23. To everyone who has an employer who is not treating you right, remember God is your vindicator. I realize it hurts every time you get passed over for a promotion to someone who doesn't work as hard as you do and put in effort. You may think that you are getting them back when you use up all your sick days, come to work and don't work but just spend the day on the internet surfing, or only putting in half the effort so the expected amount of work is not achieved. All these things may feel go to your flesh, but remember you are working unto God, not man. The Bible says, "Dearly beloved, avenge not yourselves, but rather give place unto wrath: for it is written, vengeance is mine, I will repay, saith the Lord."–Romans 12:19. For those of you who just want to coast through life and have someone else take care of you whether that is a family member you're living with and you're in your forties or older, a friend, or the government you are cheating and collecting money from your day will come as well. The Bible says, "Whatsoever thy hand findeth to do, do it with thy might; for there is no work, nor device, nor knowledge, nor wisdom, in the grave, whither thou goest."–Ecclesiastes 9:10.

S = Self-Control, do you have control over your feelings and emotions? Hopefully, you are, and you are not someone who just goes buck wild when things don't work out in their favor. Some people just go off on an angry tantrum, but then there are those that have crossed the line and caused major destruction. Hopefully, you are not one of those where that destructive downward spiral landed you in jail, but if you are just know that God still loves you and you can repent and still have success. Salvador Sabino had a tumultuous life. By the time he was 11 years old, he had already witnessed four murders. He was raised in the Dominican Republic but came to America when he was thirteen years old. Unfortunately, he hung with the wrong crowd and began selling drugs, robbing people, and fighting. Soon enough, he got locked up for armed robbery and drug possession. This turn of events was a blessing in disguise for him. He turned his life around and is now Pastor Salvador Sabino of the Heavenly Vision Christian Church in Bronx, NY. He is married with two children. The Bible says, "He that hath no rule over his own spirit is like a city that is broken down, and without walls."–Proverbs 25:28

S = Scrupulous, are you a thorough person? To have success, you must be a diligent person. Someone who pays attention to details. The story of Elisha in the bible is a true story of diligence. In the Bible, the Prophet Elijah was told by God that Elisha would succeed him once he passed away and was taken up into heaven and so Elijah went to recruit Elisha. Bible scholars believe Elisha was with Elijah for six years before Elijah was taken up in heaven. Elijah and Elisha traveled from Gilgal to Bethel and Elijah said to Elisha, "Stay here Elisha, the Lord has sent me to Jericho. And he replied, "As surely as the Lord lives and as you live. I will not leave you." So, they went to Jericho. –2 Kings 2:4. Elisha refused to leave his mentor Elijah knowing that soon he would pass away, and he would be the next prophet. Elisha was determined to be as great a prophet as Elijah was and he not only wanted to perform as many miracles as Elijah did, but he asked him if when he was called home to heaven if he would give him a double portion of his spirit. Elisha was a man who was very thorough and attentive to details. He knew how many miracles Elijah had done, and he wanted to do more. That's why he asked for a double portion of his spirit. If you want to do great things for the kingdom of God and you desire to have success, you will need to be a scrupulous person and then God will grant you, his anointing.

God Is In The Catapulting Business

Catapulting - hurling or launching (something) in a specified direction. https://www.encyclopedia.com/social-sciences-and-law/political-scien ce-and-government/military-affairs-nonnaval/catapult

GOD can and will bless you and catapult you years ahead regarding your desires. Whatever you are dreaming, wishing, and praying for, GOD can and will make it happen in record time. Or like the Star Trek fans (Trekkies) call it Warp Speed! A little one shall become a thousand, and a small one a powerful nation: I the Lord will hasten it in his time. –Isaiah 60:22. GOD wants to pour out his spirit and empower you. Our heavenly father wants to launch you forward into your destiny. God wants to launch you at lightning speed! We work on an earthly time schedule, which is the exact opposite of GOD. For GOD, a thousand years are like a day. Faith shapes GOD'S time schedule. Faith makes GOD catapult you. "There is something about believing God that will cause him to pass over a million people to get to you." - Smith Wigglesworth.

We find one of the greatest Bible stories of God catapulting someone in the Book of Esther. She was a Hebrew, and she lived in ancient Persia. As the story states, one day, the king of Persia held a lavish party and near the close of the party, he called for his wife, Queen Vashti, to come and join him. The queen refused, and the king felt humiliated. The king's men advised him he needed to banish the queen forever, and he needed to look for another wife. They brought several fair young virgins to the palace and went through a twelve-month purification process, and then each one was brought before the king for him to choose one to be his new wife. Esther's cousin Mordecai had Esther brought to the palace as well and, ultimately, she was chosen as the new Queen. Awhile after Mordecai found out about a plot to assassinate the king and advised Esther of it and she spoke about it and the plot was thwarted and they gave praise to Mordecai, and he became a minor official in the Persian government.

The king's highest official, who was named Haman, hated the Jewish people, especially Mordecai, and expected him to bow down to Haman. Haman came up with a plan to kill all the Jewish people after Mordecai refused. Mordecai found out about the plot and advised Esther of the plot to annihilate all the Jews. Mordecai then said to Esther, "Think not with thyself that thou shalt escape in the king's house, more than all the Jews. For if thou altogether holdest thy peace at this time, then shall there enlargement and deliverance arise to the Jews from another place; but thou and thy father's house shall be destroyed: and who knoweth whether thou art come to the kingdom for such a time as this? –Esther 4:13-14.

Esther urged all the Jewish people to fast and pray as she did. She spoke to the king about having a party and he agreed. At this party is where Esther revealed she was Jewish and the plot that Haman devised to kill all the Jewish people. The king became enraged and ordered Haman to be sent to the gallows and be killed. Now the interesting part here is that Haman had the same gallows he was killed on built to kill Mordecai. Remember what we spoke about in an earlier chapter leave the vindication to God he will repay. Mordecai was promoted to Haman's position, and the Jews were protected and saved.

The time frame from Esther becoming queen to when she was advised by Mordecai of the plot to kill the Jews was only three years. Look how quick God catapulted Esther from being an unknown to becoming queen to being the person who could save all the Jews' lives. GOD is waiting to get faith from you and then you will be catapulted into your dreams. Do you want to manage a team of 100 people, start your own successful business, become a successful playwright, be a New York Times bestselling author, pay off your home early? The desires are endless. It is important that you do your part and GOD will do his part. Therefore, it is imperative that You have Faith and GOD will do the Catapulting.

Overcome & Overflow

Every one of us in life at one time or another had to overcome something. A big one that everyone has had to deal with is FEAR. Whether it was a fear of heights, speaking in public, fear of being confined or in crowded places, fear of thunder and lightning, and a host of others. To become successful and live a life of thriving, you will have to overcome many things to enter that life of overflow.

It is amazing how God has set the tone for us from birth. The way to tackle anything is to take it one step at a time. When a baby learns to walk, they take one step at a time. Sure, they fall but eventually, they can take a least 2-3 steps at one time before they fall again. Parents will help them back up and set them on course to make more steps. The same thing applies in adulthood. You must take it one step at a time.

If you are looking to become a librarian, you will need to get a bachelor's degree, then a master's degree in library science, preferably from an American Library Association (ALA) program. In total, it may take you 5-6 years to reach your goal. Top librarians can earn as much as $76,000.00 per year. Well, the overcome in this situation is enduring the 5-6 years of schooling and the overflow is the salary. If you are interested in becoming a public speaker and are nervous when you must speak to large crowds of people, then you probably need to become involved with a group called Toastmasters International where you will have to do public speaking to help build your communication and leadership skills and dissolve your fear of speaking in public. Jack Canfield is an entrepreneur, author, and motivational speaker who has received between $30,000.00 - $50,000.00 per speaking engagement.

Bethany Hamilton is a professional surfer who started surfing at a young age and in 1996 she entered her first event The Rell Sunn Menehune Surfing Championship in Australia and won coming in 1st place. In 2002, she also won The Open Women's Division of the NSSA in the US coming in 1st place. Her life took a nasty turn in 2003 when she was attacked by a 14ft Tiger Shark who bit off her left arm, severing it off just below the shoulder. Once she made it to the hospital and into the ER, she'd lost over 60% of blood and was in hypovolemic shock. Even though the rains fell on her, God was with her because she was sent into surgery immediately because her father switched places with her since he was already at the hospital waiting to have knee surgery. Bethany was released from the hospital one week later and determined to not let this situation make her fearful she was back on a surfboard three weeks later. The next year in 2004 she won The NSSA National Competition in Australia coming in 1st place and then again in 2005 she won The NSSA National Competition in the US coming in 1st place. In 2007 Bethany won The NSSA Regionals and The T&C Pipeline Women's Pro both events for the US and coming in 1st place for both. Since then, she has competed and won many surfing events. She is the author of eight books, the first one published back in 2004. In 2012, she met a youth pastor named Adam Dirks, and they got engaged in 2013 and then married later in 2013. They now have three sons and are blessed. Bethany attributes her strength to her Christian faith. This is a prime example of overcome & overflow.

Whatever you are looking to overcome the Bible with God's word is the authority on it:

Anxiety & Worry– "Be strong and of a good courage, fear not, nor be afraid of them: for the Lord thy God, he it is that doth go with thee; he will not fail thee, nor forsake thee." -Deuteronomy 31:6

Depression– "The eyes of the Lord are upon the righteous, and his ears are open unto their cry. The righteous cry, and the Lord heareth, and delivereth them out of all their troubles."–Psalm 34:15 & 17

Discouragement & Despair– "Therefore we do not become discouraged [spiritless, disappointed, or afraid]. Though our outer self is [progressively] wasting away, yet our inner self is being [progressively] renewed day by day. For our momentary, light distress [this passing trouble] is producing for us an eternal weight of glory [a fullness] beyond all measure [surpassing all comparisons, a transcendent splendor and an endless blessedness]!" -2 Corinthians 4:16-17.

Fear– "The Lord is my light and my salvation; whom shall I fear? The Lord is the strength of my life; of whom shall I be afraid?" - Psalms 27:1

Insecurity: "Fear thou not; for I am with thee be not dismayed; for I am thy God: I will strengthen thee; yea, I will help thee; yea, I will uphold thee with the right hand of my righteousness." -Isaiah 41:10

Stress– "Be careful for nothing; but in everything by prayer and supplication with thanksgiving let your requests be made known unto God." -Philippians 4:6

Temptations– "In the day when I called, you answered me; and You strengthened me with strength (might and inflexibility to temptation) in my inner self." -Psalms 138:3

God has planned an abundant overflow life for all of us. He said so in his word, "The thief comes only in order to steal and kill and destroy. I came that they may have and enjoy life, and have it in abundance (to the full, till it [a]overflows)."–John 10:10. We just must do our part, which is to overcome and then the overflow will stream like rivers of water.

Manifestation

Manifestation - the act, process, or an instance of manifesting. A perceptible, outward, or visible expression. http://www.wickipedia.com

Are you waiting for a manifestation, or maybe several, to happen in your life? Have you been praying unceasingly daily? Have you waited so long that you have just given up hope? Well, I have good news for you. Don't give up hope because you are not alone.

Even with automation like toll booths, where you have a device in your car that electronically communicates with the toll booth when there is no attendant to process your payment and keep you moving. In today's day and age 24/7 fast food service, there are still times you have several cars in line ahead of you and you must wait to receive your order. Waiting for all of us is inevitable. Also, believe it or not, we must wait more often than we think. Of course, sometimes we know we will have to wait no matter what. A pregnant mother waiting to give birth to her baby, boarding a plane with other people, and waiting on the runway to taxi for takeoff, whatever fruit or vegetable seeds you have planted in your garden to grow and produce.

Manifestation is all about waiting and for most of us, that is sometimes a daunting task, especially if you are a Type A personality like myself. We want it done and we want it done yesterday. Then we realize the timing does not depend on us it depends on God and so we mellow some. Then our feathers get ruffled again because it is taking too long. Well, how long is too long? Let's look at some examples from the bible.

Abraham–God promised Abraham that he would be the father of many nations. When God said that Abraham and his wife Sarah did not have any children. They waited many years until Sarah convinced Abraham to have a child with her handmaid. The child was born and named Ishmael, but this was not the child God promised. At 100, Abraham and Sarah 90 finally had the child God promised, and they named him Isaac. Abraham waited 25 years.

Joseph–God spoke to Joseph in a dream and told him he would become a powerful man and reign over many, including his older brothers. He said that dream to his siblings and that angered them and so they threw him into a pit. A caravan of Ishmaelites found him in the pit and took him to Egypt and sold him to Potiphar, the captain of Pharaoh's guard. Potiphar's wife made sexual advances on Joseph, which he rebuked and so she lied about him trying to take advantage of her and was thrown in jail. Finally, when Pharoah needed an interpretation of a dream, he called for Joseph to be brought to him. He told Joseph the dream, and he interpreted it and was released by Pharoah and was promoted to chief administrator of Egypt second to Pharoah. From the time God gave Joseph the dream until it was manifested was 13 years.

Job–God allowed the devil to destroy everything that Job had so he could prove Job's faithfulness to God. Job was a very wealthy man. He lost everything, including his wife and children. Job trusted God and remained faithful through it all. In the end, when Job had passed the test, God restored twice the amount of what Job originally had lost in cattle, property, children, crops, and children. Job had patience.

Don't worry ladies, I did not forget about you.

Hannah–In the Book of Samuel, there is a story about a young woman named Hannah. She was married to a man named Elkanah, and they were very much in love. Hannah, however, could not have children and after many tries, she convinced her husband Elkanah to take another wife named Peninnah, who gave birth to several sons and daughters for him. However, Elkanah did not love Peninnah the way he loved Hannah, and that drove Peninnah to jealousy. She taunted Hannah mercilessly about being barren, but Hannah kept her dignity and grace and held her tongue and continued to pray to God for a child. One day while Hannah was at the temple, she was so despondent and explained to the priest Eli what was troubling her. She said she will give up her child if she ever had one that she would dedicate him to the church. God was so pleased with Hannah's patience and perseverance that she had a son and named him Samuel. She kept him until he was 3 years old and then gave him to the church. She kept in contact visiting him and watched him grow. God blessed her patience by giving her 5 more children, three sons, and two daughters.

Esther–She was a young Jewish woman who was being raised by her cousin Mordecai. She was obedient and beautiful. Her cousin sent her to become a part of the King Ahasuerus harem. She finds favor with the king and becomes the queen. Her cousin Mordecai uncovers a plot to kill all the Jews and tells her she must speak with the king to save her people. Once getting informed of the plot to kill the Jews, she becomes frightened and is overcome with helplessness. She may not see the king unless they summoned her. She goes to the king unsummoned and explains her plight. He resolves to save her people and kill the one who orchestrated this plot. Esther showed her faithfulness and belief in God that he would save her people if she did her part. God provided the manifestation for her.

Ruth–She is the daughter-in-law of Naomi. We have compared Naomi to a female Job. She lost her home, husband, and children. Some say she lost even more than Job did. When Naomi's and Ruth's husband died, Naomi advised Ruth to go on and live her life, but Ruth was a loyal woman and stayed with Naomi. Ruth had great faith. Her faith and belief in God that he would provide for Naomi and herself was solid. They introduced Ruth to a man named Boaz, and she proved to be a woman of integrity with Boaz. Ruth went to go work in the fields of a man named Boaz. Boaz was a single wealthy man. Boaz fell in love with Ruth, and she went from a lowly field worker to being Boaz's wife. The book of Ruth shows the workings of divine providence. The book reveals the extent of God's grace. God blessed Ruth and manifested to her exceedingly and abundantly. God fully accepted Ruth into His elect people and recognized her with a role in continuing the family line into which his appointed king, David, and later His Son, Jesus, would be born. After Boaz married Ruth, she became pregnant and had a son named Obed. This man, Obed, became the father of Jesse. Now Jesse was the father of David, who was in the direct family line of Jesus Christ.

Are you waiting for your manifestation? Patience is the key. We are always in a hurry and God is not. God's timing is often a mystery. He doesn't do things on our timetable. However, the Bible promises God will not be late, not one day. "For the vision is yet for an appointed time, but at the end, it shall speak, and not lie: though it tarry, wait for it; because it will surely come, it will not tarry."–Habakkuk 2:3.

God's Promises

Anxiety

1-Casting all your care upon him; for he careth for you. -1 Peter 5:7.

2-When thou passest through the waters, I will be with thee; and through the rivers, they shall not overflow thee: when thou walkest through the fire, thou shalt not be burned; neither shall the flame kindle upon thee. –Isaiah 43:2

3-Many sorrows shall be to the wicked: but he that trusteth in the Lord, mercy shall compass him about. –Psalm 32:10

Contentment

1-But seek ye first the kingdom of God, and his righteousness; and all these things shall be added unto you. –Matthew 6:33

2-But my God shall supply all your need according to his riches in glory by Christ Jesus. -Philippians 4:19

Courage

1-Be strong and of a good courage, fear not, nor be afraid of them: for the Lord thy God, he it is that doth go with thee; he will not fail thee, nor forsake thee. -Deuteronomy 31:6

2-Wait on the Lord: be of good courage, and he shall strengthen thine heart: wait, I say, on the Lord. –Psalms 27:14

Depression

1-The righteous cry, and the Lord heareth, and delivereth them out of all their troubles. –Psalms 34:17

2-Many are the afflictions of the righteous: but the Lord delivereth him out of them all. –Psalms 34:19

3-The Lord also will be a refuge for the oppressed, a refuge in times of trouble. –Psalms 9:9

Faith

1-And Jesus answering saith unto them, Have faith in God. For verily I say unto you, that whosoever shall say unto this mountain, be thou removed, and be thou cast into the sea; and shall not doubt in his heart but shall believe that those things which he saith shall come to pass; he shall have whatsoever he saith. Therefore, I say unto you, what things soever ye desire, when ye pray, believe that ye receive them, and ye shall have them. -Mark 11:22-24

2- For with God nothing shall be impossible. –Luke 1:37

Favor

1-For the Lord God is a sun and shield: the Lord will give grace and glory: no good thing will he withhold from them that walk uprightly. –Psalms 84:11

2-And the Lord shall guide thee continually, and satisfy thy soul in drought, and make fat thy bones: and thou shalt be like a watered garden, and like a spring of water, whose waters fail not. –Isaiah 58:11

3-The curse of the Lord is in the house of the wicked: but he blesseth the habitation of the just. Surely, he scorneth the scorners: but he giveth grace unto the lowly. The wise shall inherit glory: but shame shall be the promotion of fools. –Proverbs 3:33-35

Fear

1-Fear thou not; for I am with thee: be not dismayed; for I am thy God: I will strengthen thee; yea, I will help thee; yea, I will uphold thee with the right hand of my righteousness. –Isaiah 41:10

2- I sought the Lord, and he heard me, and delivered me from all my fears. –Psalm 34:4

3-The fear of the Lord tendeth to life: and he that hath it shall abide satisfied; he shall not be visited with evil. –Proverbs 19:23

Forgiveness

1-If we confess our sins, he is faithful and just to forgive us our sins, and to cleanse us from all unrighteousness. –1 John 1:9.

2- For if ye forgive men their trespasses, your heavenly Father will also forgive you. –Matthew 6:14

3-Judge not, and ye shall not be judged: condemn not, and ye shall not be condemned: forgive, and ye shall be forgiven. –Luke 6:37

Health

1-Beloved, I wish above all things that thou mayest prosper and be in health, even as thy soul prospereth. –3 John 1:2.

2-For I will restore health unto thee, and I will heal thee of thy wounds, saith the Lord. –Jeremiah 30:17

3-Behold, I will bring it health and cure, and I will cure them, and will reveal unto them the abundance of peace and truth. –Jeremiah 33:6

4-Who his own self bare our sins in his own body on the tree, that we, being dead to sins, should live unto righteousness: by whose stripes ye were healed. –1 Peter 2:24.

5-And the prayer of faith shall save the sick, and the Lord shall raise him up; and if he have committed sins, they shall be forgiven him. –James 5:15

6-Bless the Lord, O my soul, and forget not all his benefits: Who forgiveth all thine iniquities; who healeth all thy diseases; Who redeemeth thy life from destruction; who crowneth thee with lovingkindness and tender mercies. – Psalms 103:2-4

7-The Lord will strengthen him upon the bed of languishing: thou wilt make all his bed in his sickness. - Psalms 41:3

8-He healeth the broken in heart, and bindeth up their wounds. –Psalms 147:3

Hope

1-Now the God of hope fill you with all joy and peace in believing, that ye may abound in hope, through the power of the Holy Ghost. – Romans 15:13

2-For I know the thoughts that I think toward you, saith the Lord, thoughts of peace, and not of evil, to give you an expected end. – Jeremiah 29:11

3-For we are saved by hope: but hope that is seen is not hope: for what a man seeth, why doth he yet hope for? –Romans 8:24

Insecurity

1-There hath no temptation taken you, but such as is common to man: but God is faithful, who will not suffer you to be tempted above that ye are able; but will with the temptation also make a way to escape, that ye may be able to bear it. –1 Corinthians 10:13.

2-If ye abide in me, and my words abide in you, ye shall ask what ye will, and it shall be done unto you. Herein is my Father glorified, that ye bear much fruit; so, shall ye be my disciples. –John 15:7-8

Integrity

1-He that walketh uprightly walketh surely: but he that perverteth his ways shall be known. –Proverbs 10:9

2-The integrity of the upright shall guide them: but the perverseness of transgressors shall destroy them. –Proverbs 11:3

3-The just man walketh in his integrity: his children are blessed after him. –Proverbs 20:7

4- Lying lips are abomination to the Lord: but they that deal truly are his delight. –Proverbs 12:22

Lonesome

1-Teaching them to observe all things whatsoever I have commanded you: and, lo, I am with you always, even unto the end of the world. Amen. –Matthew 28:20.

2-When my father and my mother forsake me, then the Lord will take me up. –Psalms 27:10

3-I will not leave you comfortless: I will come to you. –John 14:18

Patience

1-And let us not be weary in well doing: for in due season we shall reap, if we faint not. –Galatians 6:9

2-Rest in the Lord and wait patiently for him: fret not thyself because of him who prospereth in his way, because of the man who bringeth wicked devices to pass. Cease from anger and forsake wrath: fret not thyself in any wise to do evil. For evildoers shall be cut off: but those that wait upon the Lord, they shall inherit the earth. –Psalms 37:7-9

3-But they that wait upon the Lord shall renew their strength; they shall mount up with wings as eagles; they shall run, and not be weary; and they shall walk, and not faint. –Isaiah 40:31

Peace

1-These things I have spoken unto you, that in me ye might have peace. In the world ye shall have tribulation: but be of good cheer; I have overcome the world. –John 16:33

2-Thou wilt keep him in perfect peace, whose mind is stayed on thee: because he trusteth in thee. –Isaiah 26:3

3-Blessed are the peacemakers: for they shall be called the children of God. –Matthew 5:9

4-For God is not the author of confusion, but of peace, as in all churches of the saints. –1 Corinthians 14:33.

Prayer

1-If ye abide in me, and my words abide in you, ye shall ask what ye will, and it shall be done unto you. –John 15:7

2-Therefore I say unto you, what things soever ye desire, when ye pray, believe that ye receive them, and ye shall have them. –Mark 11:24

3-But thou, when thou prayest, enter into thy closet, and when thou hast shut thy door, pray to thy Father which is in secret; and thy Father which seeth in secret shall reward thee openly. –Matthew 6:6

4-And I say unto you, Ask, and it shall be given you; seek, and ye shall find; knock, and it shall be opened unto you. –Luke 11:9

5-Call unto me, and I will answer thee, and show thee great and mighty things, which thou knowest not. –Jeremiah 33:3

Prosperity

1-But thou shalt remember the Lord thy God: for it is he that giveth thee power to get wealth, that he may establish his covenant which he sware unto thy fathers, as it is this day. -Deuteronomy 8:18

2-But my God shall supply all your need according to his riches in glory by Christ Jesus. -Philippians 4:19

3-Bring ye all the tithes into the storehouse, that there may be meat in mine house, and prove me now herewith, saith the Lord of hosts, if I will not open you the windows of heaven, and pour you out a blessing, that there shall not be room enough to receive it. –Malachi 3:10

4- Beloved, I wish above all things that thou mayest prosper and be in health, even as thy soul prospereth. –3 John 1:2.

5-For thou shalt eat the labour of thine hands: happy shalt thou be, and it shall be well with thee. –Psalms 128:2

6-And God is able to make all grace abound toward you; that ye, always having all sufficiency in all things, may abound to every good work. –2 Corinthians 9:8.

7- And he shall be like a tree planted by the rivers of water, that bringeth forth his fruit in his season; his leaf also shall not wither; and whatsoever he doeth shall prosper. –Psalms 1:3

8-Give, and it shall be given unto you; good measure, pressed down, and shaken together, and running over, shall men give into your bosom. For with the same measure that ye mete withal it shall be measured to you again. –Luke 6:38.

Protection

1-The angel of the Lord encampeth round about them that fear him, and delivereth them. –Psalms 34:7

2-God is our refuge and strength, a very present help in trouble. -Psalms 46:1

3-As the mountains are round about Jerusalem, so the Lord is round about his people from henceforth even forever. –Psalms 125:2

4- But the Lord is faithful, who shall stablish you, and keep you from evil. - 2 Thessalonians 3:3

5-No weapon that is formed against thee shall prosper; and every tongue that shall rise against thee in judgment thou shalt condemn. This is the heritage of the servants of the Lord, and their righteousness is of me, saith the Lord. –Isaiah 54:17.

Stress

1-Cast thy burden upon the Lord, and he shall sustain thee: he shall never suffer the righteous to be moved. –Psalms 55:22

2-I called upon the Lord in distress: the Lord answered me and set me in a large place. –Psalms 118:5

3-And we know that all things work together for good to them that love God, to them who are the called according to his purpose. –Romans 8:28

4-What shall we then say to these things? If God be for us, who can be against us? –Romans 8:31.

5- He is like a man which built an house, and digged deep, and laid the foundation on a rock: and when the flood arose, the stream beat vehemently upon that house, and could not shake it: for it was founded upon a rock. –Luke 6:48

6-Cast thy burden upon the Lord, and he shall sustain thee: he shall never suffer the righteous to be moved. –Psalms 55:22

7-The righteous cry, and the Lord heareth, and delivereth them out of all their troubles. The Lord is nigh unto them that are of a broken heart; and saveth such as be of a contrite spirit. Many are the afflictions of the righteous: but the Lord delivereth him out of them all. –Psalms 34:17-19

Trust

1-Trust in the Lord with all thine heart; and lean not unto thine own understanding. In all thy ways acknowledge him, and he shall direct thy paths. –Proverbs 3:5-6

2- Commit thy way unto the Lord; trust also in him; and he shall bring it to pass. –Psalms 37:5

3-For I know the thoughts that I think toward you, saith the Lord, thoughts of peace, and not of evil, to give you an expected end. –Jeremiah 29:11

Victory

1-For the Lord your God is he that goeth with you, to fight for you against your enemies, to save you. -Deuteronomy 20:4

2-Through God we shall do valiantly: for he it is that shall tread down our enemies. –Psalms 108:13

3-But thanks be to God, which giveth us the victory through our Lord Jesus Christ. -1 Corinthians 15:57

4-For whatsoever is born of God overcometh the world: and this is the victory that overcometh the world, even our faith. –1 John 5:4.

5- And he said unto me, It is done. I am Alpha and Omega, the beginning and the end. I will give unto him that is athirst of the fountain of the water of life freely. He that overcometh shall inherit all things; and I will be his God, and he shall be my son. –Revelations 21:6-7

Epilogue

I am very honored and humbled to have been given the opportunity by God to write this book for everyone. I pray this book will be a blessing for everyone's life and that you will realize several things:

Life is a journey and no matter how many high wire balancing acts you may encounter or cliff hangers, life presents to you, remember God is with you all the way.

Tests come to all of us and the sooner we realize the ones that keep getting repeated and just pass them, the smoother the journey will become.

Challenges and Trials will come to all of us, but this is when we must stay in faith, believe, & trust God always. If you never have any tests you will never have a testimony to tell that someone else can hear that will help them with their journey.

Keep God as a mainline, not a sideline.

Stop fighting everything. Some things mature you and strengthen you. You cannot pray bold prayers to God, but never expect to encounter any challenges and trials. God needs to make sure you are ready for the exceeding and abundant overflow he has coming your way.

Yes, the rain falls on the just and the unjust but remember because you are a believer and a child of God the Bible says, "The name of the Lord is a strong tower: the righteous runneth into it and is safe."–Proverbs 18:10.

Remember the words of King David: "The Lord is my rock, and my fortress, and my deliverer; my God, my strength, in whom I will trust; my buckler, and the horn of my salvation, and my high tower."–Psalms 18:2.

About Donna Louis

Raised in New York Donna has always had a penchant for writing. Constantly surrounded by pen and paper Donna studied writing courses at Queensboro Community College in New York. She attended The Institute of Children's Writers and Long Ridge Writers Group in Connecticut. She moved to Florida and because of her relationship with The Holy Spirit she wrote a book on miracles.

Donna's first book Miracles of Direction Miracles of Conquest Miracles of Provision Miracles of Purpose helped readers explore miracles both past and present. The book explores biblical miracles that took place while Jesus was here on earth. She then references with miracles that take place daily in the modern world. She separates these miracles into four categories and presents insightful examples of each type, taken directly from the Bible.

They chose her as the winner in the 2018 Top Female Author Awards in the Religion/Philosophy/Spiritual category from The Author Show. They chose Donna from an international field of contestants by a panel of judges. They also chose her as a winner in 50 Great Writers You Should Be Reading in 2015, 2016, 2017 and 2018.

Donna Louis' second book best-selling book, 'Thriving in Every Season of Life with God', gives us a road map to create a mindset - a new life in which we can learn to prosper in any circumstance, however dire. The book achieved bestseller status in two categories: Spiritual Self Help and Motivational Self Help.

Donna's third book best-selling book, "Book of Proverbs – Proverbs For The Modern Day" provides intellectual depth, insights, and exceptional wisdom on how to live a meaningful, joyful, and tranquil life by honoring and respecting God as omnipotent. The book achieved best seller status in six categories: Christian Inspiration, Christian Devotionals, Christian Living, Religion & Spirituality, Christian E-Books & Bibles & Christian Spiritual Growth.

Donna Louis also has new videos for her Motivational Mondays With Donna available every Monday on her YouTube channel https://www.youtube.com/channel/UCJCieSU2FYdC09F3YNkfzDw..

Donna has been married to her husband of 38 years Patrick Louis and lives in Florida. She lives to accomplish the task that God created her for and daily to follow Proverbs 3:5-6. "Trust in the Lord with all thine heart and lean not unto thine own understanding. In all thy ways acknowledge him, and he shall direct thy paths."

www.ingramcontent.com/pod-product-compliance
Lightning Source LLC
Chambersburg PA
CBHW070205160726
47997CB00017B/438